"*Servants & Spies* reads like a th

anything but fiction. What migh

exploding bullet, Mike Kastle's story begins with a bang quickly drawing the reader into a fascinating plot combining intrigue with inspiration. Having been a missionary in Mozambique, I can say that Kastle's adventures in a Marxist world are not the typical life of most missionaries. Danger lurks around every corner, but his experiences also include the opportunity to influence China with the secret message of Jesus. His stories are compelling and genuine, illustrating in vivid detail the difference one can make when he dedicates his life to God's purposes. What you spend to purchase this book will quadruple in value with each page you read."

—DON MILAM, Acquisitions Consultant, *Whitaker House*
Author, *Ancient Language of Eden*

"Wow.... A beautifully written documentation of actual events. It reads like fiction, but I personally know it is not. Having worked with Mike daily for over 10 years, I had the privilege to witness some of the stories he writes about as they were happening. They are even more powerful reading his recollection of the events. I was impressed with his ability to remember them so clearly. The stories confirm his integrity and truthfulness. I would often tell Mike that, "He didn't just profess to be a Christian, but that he was Christian-like in the way that he lived his life." Reading this book has solidified that belief. It is his embodiment of Christianity that distinguishes his actions."

—RONALD J. SORRENTINO, R.Ph., MBA, Field Vice-President
(retired), *GlaxoSmithKine (GSK), North American Pharmaceuticals*

"*Servants & Spies* is the witness of one man's journey in being faithful and tested before the Lord. The call of a Christian is to step out on faith and continual growth in understanding how each of us can be a part of His eternal plan if only we are courageous to listen and obey. Mike Kastle's intriguing story provides the reader not only an easy to read page-turner, but an underlying deep message to challenge and guide every Christian in his or her walk. Servants & Spies is a must-read for anyone seeking to serve the Lord more and trapped in his or her fears that they are not enough. Mike's collection of real-life experiences demonstrate that God can use what talents you come with and further equip you in areas you never thought possible... all it takes is to the courage to step out on faith and trust in His plan."

—CHRISTOPHER L. COOK, *PharmD, PhD*
Head, *US Medical Affairs*
bioMérieux, Inc.

SERVANTS & SPIES

Servants & Spies: *exploits from the covert mission field*

ISBN: 9798671020366

A Publication of Tall Pine Books

|| *tallpinebooks.com*

*Printed in the United States of America

SERVANTS & SPIES

EXPLOITS FROM THE COVERT MISSION FIELD

MIKE KASTLE

Tall Pine

To Mike, my best friend and fellow servant of the Lord. I miss you.
We will see you again on that day!

ACKNOWLEDGMENTS

My utmost thanks to my wonderful wife, whose encouragement, patience, love and help have been infinite. Your eagerness to serve, and your willingness to walk together with me in the challenging places and paths unknown, provide glaring evidence of your devotion to the Lord and compassion for others. I love you more than anything in this world, and I'm so proud to be your husband.

Good leaders equip us, motivate us, and help us to make wise decisions. But great leaders challenge us and change our lives! Many thanks to the Great leadership of my spiritual Dad, who taught me more about the Great Commission through his heart and life than I could have learned from a thousand books and sermons (but, of course, his books and sermons are great too!).

To the many other great people who have encouraged me in writing this book, including my friends, extended family and overseas staff, I sincerely thank you for your wisdom, creativity and willingness to use your gifts and skills for the glory of our Lord.

Many thanks to the publishing team of Tall Pine Books, and to my writing coach, Don Milam, who have encouraged me and have provided insightful input and creative ideas throughout the process.

CONTENTS

FOREWORD

I first met Mike Kastle at a large public conference we were hosting designed for empowering Christians to live a more fully enriched and supernatural life. A focus of the meetings was also for physical healing which we had been of part of ministering for many years around the world. I had noticed a particular man in the audience who sat in rapt attention. There was something so different about him I had a distinct urge to find out more.

Between sessions I approached and as I came near I noticed his conference badge with a rather usual American name and a place of origin I dared not even try to pronounce. The two seemed impossibly paired. When Mike told me where he was from and how he had come from the other side of the world to our conference I discovered that he was mutual acquaintances with our spiritual mentor of many years. As Mike described the nature of his work I was extremely curious. Either he was exaggerating or he and his wife were living on the fold of human experience that lies between the natural and supernatural, temporal and eternal, realms. Mike carried himself so unassuming and soft spoken, yet there was a presence and joyful confidence about him that was remarkable. There seemed to be much more beneath the surface so I quietly asked one of our staff members to find out more. In fact, to see if he was legit and if so to arrange for him to meet us and the other speakers and spend some time in fellowship. Little did we know that meeting was prearranged for reasons that would impact the lives and eternity of people on the opposite side of the globe we would never meet this side of heaven.

How does a normal guy with a wife and children who suits up as a corporate lawyer and goes to the office in middle America become an emissary of medical supplies and personnel, living by faith in a land of many languages, slipping in and out of foreign countries filled with need as an under-the-radar messenger of hope and healing? Mike has learned the meaning and method of living a purpose filled life. He has practiced and succeeded at doing the impossible by taking simple steps of faith one at a time. He has discovered that God invites each of us to embark on the ultimate quest of love and friendship, of challenge and conquest. He has gained the knowledge of taking faith the size of a mustard seed and growing a tree that provides shelter and healing for thousands and will grow into the next generations. Mike Kastle is a man on a mission.

You may not realize that what you are holding in your hands is a passport. *Servants & Spies* is the answer to prayers you've prayed and some you would never dream or dare to pray. Like a modern day Abraham, who went out from everything familiar to possess an inheritance he never imagined, like Saul of Tarsus who left for a certain city intent upon his own plan until his encounter with a Person of pure light on the road changed him and changed his reason for living, like two brothers who only knew fishing until an invitation from a Stranger called them to be fishers of men, Mike Kastle's true story has come to you by divine plan. It comes not just from Mike, but from the One who calls you to adventure, for you to consider that far country called the kingdom of God and all the benefits of living fully as a resident there, and, as its ambassador delivering those benefits to people who have not yet enjoyed them.

Servants & Spies is a gift to all who seek those riches. In it Mike takes us step-by-step on his epic journey of discovery. He faithfully takes us into his world, shows us his frailties, shares his talents, and freely gives us keys of know-how he paid a great price for. Within these pages the Spirit of God draws an illustrated map, instructions for preparations and planning, a practical handbook on recognizing and hearing God's voice, and following. Mike's journey from corporate lawyer to servant and spy serves as a living guidebook that will help you see all the planned and coincidental moments, meetings, and experience of your life, past and present, are the beautiful pieces of predetermined purpose and destiny. Let's go!

—BONNIE CHAVDA
Sr. Pastor & Co-Founder *The Watch of the Lord*
All Nations Church and Healing Center
Ft. Mill, South Carolina

PREFACE

Ministry is more than just a position we hold or the work and service that we perform. Instead, it is the very essence and reflection of Jesus' love, through us, to a lost and hurting world.

Many of us may have a sense that God has called us to serve Him. But, we may sometimes be unsure and ask, "Exactly how do I walk in this calling?" *and* "When do I begin?"

I was working as a lawyer in a successful career when the Lord called me to change the course of our family's lives and work for Him full-time. I, too, didn't know the answer to these questions, and I had received some conflicting advice from others.

Some said to me that the call to ministry is difficult, so if there is anything I could do other than that, I should. They also noted that if the Lord compelled me forward in the ministry, I would know it is Him. Others said that I must plan out my education and ministry career pathway and stick with it, without distraction. One church leader even told me that ministry is only valid if it involves church planting or evangelism. Maybe you have received this sort of advice also. Perhaps the best advice I received was from a senior missionary from Britain who told me that I simply must, "Find out what God wants you to do, and do it."

Servants & Spies walks us through what it means when God begins to call us to His work and shows by example how He shapes us, prepares us, and helps to build the foundation necessary for what He alone has called us to do. Together we learn how the Lord's purpose and plan for our ministry develops in our lives using real-life examples from the very beginning of a ministry to its most fruitful stages, including examples of how He changes us and uses everything about us and everything we do, for His glory.

May you be encouraged to hold Him close as He amazes you on the incredible journey ahead, because, as you will soon learn, your ministry begins before you know it!

PART I

1

IT BEGINS BEFORE WE KNOW IT

"For I know the plans I have for you, declares the LORD, plans to prosper you and not to harm you, plans to give you hope and a future." (Jeremiah. 29:11)

"It is the glory of God to conceal a matter; to search out a matter is the glory of kings." (Proverbs 25:2)

NEVER DID I expect a gun to my head! Aimed right at my forehead! *Really!? Really!?* I knew it was possible that this could happen, but I didn't expect it and certainly not this soon! I had prepared for this trip for months and we had a great plan in place... but was it going to end before it even began?

I had been to North Korea a few months prior, and this was a follow-up trip. The first trip was far more dangerous. Yet, this time, things escalated quickly. I rounded the corner at the North Korea border entry-station, after exiting China. I was ready to show them my approval documents so I could enter the country yet again. The North Korean customs guard gave me a not-so-welcoming gesture to come through the security gate. *And then the gun.* I wasn't afraid; I was just surprised. I knew that we should always expect the unexpected while on a mission, but I wasn't prepared for this situation.

I quickly realized it was merely an infrared temperature gauge shaped like a gun. *What a relief.* The guard had pointed it directly at my forehead to take my body-temperature. It was very up-close and personal. I don't think he realized how aggressive this gesture seemed to outsiders entering into North Korea, especially with his unwelcoming demeanor. I could tell he was not happy to greet an American.

North Korea and America are still under a formal declaration of war, but it has been stalled since 1953 by an Armistice agreement. This stall has done little in the minds of the North Koreans to give assurance of their safety among the foreign "enemies" of the United States. Yet there I was, as an American, face to face with the government administrative official. Needless to say, he was not happy to see me.

The reason he decided to take my temperature was because they needed to ensure that all who enter their country not only have the requisite approval, but also that they are healthy and would not bring sicknesses in with them. After all, their country is already starved of good medical care. I could understand that. He was just doing his job. I responded kindly to him, reflecting the fact that I was safe in the Kingdom of God regardless of where I was on earth. I was safe indeed, but nevertheless, my senses were now on full alert and I was fully engaged for what might come next!

We crossed the border for this second trip into North Korea just two months after our first one. We entered into the country through its north-eastern border with China. At that time, the border between North Korea and China was distinct, but it was slightly porous due to the scarcity of fencing, not to mention certain types of trade had been common among the North Koreans and the Chinese.

We had left our cell phones and most of our personal belongings with trusted friends in China and planned to retrieve them when we returned a few days later. Our families were praying non-stop for our safety and for a successful mission. Just one day earlier, I had bid farewell to my son, David, who had joined me on a separate mission in China. He was now headed back home to the USA as I was headed for North Korea. I still carry in my heart the look of concern on his face just the day before when he wondered whether or not he would see his dad again.

It was very unusual for Americans to visit North Korea. This was before the country had opened its borders to organized tours. So, our work was highly scrutinized by the North Korean government, and we were watched closely—we knew we would be. I had invited a friend from the United States to accompany me on this trip and it was an exciting venture for him, as well. We could only talk freely when we were alone, which was a seldom occasion. Most of the time, we were accompanied by a government security agent who carried a device to record all of our conversations along the way. He also held our passports and, from time to time, questioned us about places that our passports revealed we had been previously. He was particularly curious about my prior trips to Kazakhstan, a former Soviet Republic. He wanted to make sure we were not spies. *Were we?*

This was an unusual mission, but I've come to understand that *all* missions are unusual, and all must be managed carefully. We stayed focused to complete what we were assigned to do. As usual, our covert assignment differed somewhat from what it appeared to be to those around us. Our real mission needed to be accomplished in private, in the shadows. We had a job to do. We were tasked to secretly lay the groundwork for what we expected would occur in the future.

North Korea was not in good shape (and it still isn't). North Korea's self-imposed isolation from the rest of the world has left its population in poverty, except for the small ruling class that enjoys the sparse wealth that does exist. Most North Koreans are farmers or merchants, and even their children are sometimes left scouring garbage dumps and empty farmer's fields looking for remnants of food.

With citizens starving for food, information, and freedoms that they can only speculate exist (due to their isolation from the world), the North Korean regime most certainly cannot continue forever in its current state. This was part of our mission. As one can imagine, it was *very* important that the guards did not know that. Our mission was to prepare a way for the Christian believers in North Korea to grow in faith and in numbers—before, during, and after the current dictatorial regime comes to an end.

We were always acutely aware of where we were. North Korea is not a normal environment, and we knew it presented both political risks and *spiritual* risks, as well. It was truly enemy territory in the spiritual sense, and we knew that the enemy would try to interfere with God's plans. North Korea's spiritual climate is more hostile than perhaps any other. In fact, when we left North Korea and crossed the border back into China, I thought, *Whew, I'm safe. I'm in China!*—a thought I never thought I would have.

A few months after we left North Korea, I was watching the news on television in my home in the United States. I was captivated by a brief flash of breaking news when the commentators announced that an American citizen was just taken captive in North Korea. They didn't give us his name yet. I quickly moved toward the TV to listen closely because this may have relevance to our ministry work there. *Wow*, I thought. *That could have been me, or one of our colleagues.* How fortunate it was that we were safe.

Shortly after the news broadcast, I received a phone call from my ministry colleague, telling me that a group of men had just been taken captive. One of the men was our friend, a Korean-American who had come into North Korea with us previously. After we left North Korea, he apparently returned back into the country for further business. They were ready and waiting for him, because, as we later learned, our "cover" had been blown. Thankfully, after months of negotiations with North Korea, through the Swedish Embassy in North Korea that was acting as the intermediary, our friend was released. However, I was informed that the North Koreans now knew who I was and they were convinced that I was either a spy or a pastor—both of which were illegal and carried a sentence of death.

OUR HISTORY IN CHINA

Our excursion into North Korea was not part of our normal mission work, which for the six prior years was centered in China. It was ordained by the Lord and was part of His ongoing work in support of the believers who love Him but can only meet in secret under threat of losing their own lives. Our work there had to be, and still must be, done in secret.

Our work in China began in 2004, and at the time of writing this book, we have been working in China for over 16 years. I'll discuss more about that throughout this book. Of course, the Lord has been working in China much longer than that, but my involvement began with an exploratory trip in 2004 when I was invited by a friend to come to China to evaluate the prospect of me bringing future teams for medical mission projects.

Our China projects have continued to grow throughout the years, and ultimately, I left my career as a lawyer and my wife and I moved to China. This leap was necessary for us in order to manage the work properly. Within ten years, our simple work, which had unexpected beginnings, has become one of the largest foreign medical outreach ministries in the whole country. This is not our doing. It is God's. This is truly His work.

Living and working in His mission field is, in some ways, the same as life in our home country–filled with new challenges and adventures daily. We are especially privileged because He allows us to see some truly amazing things! Sometimes things don't go as expected; He always surprises us.

Once, we were hosting a medical team in a remote Muslim-village in a northwest Chinese region. That afternoon, a village woman brought her ten-day-old baby to us, desperately seeking our help. The poor baby was so limp and sick. He was gasping for air. His abdomen muscle wall had not closed before birth, so his internal organs were visible—and were visibly infected.

Although our team was equipped for surgery, we were not equipped for critical care and the only thing I could offer was to pray. Open prayer in this Muslim environment was not safe, so we took the mother and baby behind one of our medical tents and I asked several others to gather around to pray. We prayed, asking the Lord for healing, and for His will to be done. Unfortunately, the baby died shortly thereafter. We were disappointed and sad. However, the Lord's work was not over.

After about thirty minutes, one of my team members came and told me that one of the local village men had been deeply touched by the situation and our prayers. Reason being, when we prayed for the baby, I had asked this man to translate my prayer for the mother from Chinese into the local language so the young mother could hear our prayers to the Lord on her behalf.

As he was translating the prayer to a God whom he didn't know and had never heard of, he was touched and asked if he could know this God. From there, he asked the Lord into his life to be saved. This was a wonderful outcome from a truly sad event. The Lord used the baby's physical death to bring spiritual life to another. Only He can do that! Praise the Lord!

That same day, while giving medical care to so many of the residents, I was struck with the compassion of the Lord for one particular young woman who came to our team for help. She was probably in her late teens or early adult years. She was completely blind. As she was waiting in line, I went up to her and brought her aside so that I could pray for her that the Lord would restore her eyes to see. I prayed for her, and afterward, she too received the Lord into her heart. Yet she did not receive her sight.

The next year, we returned to the same village with another medical team. It was not our normal practice to serve the same village twice. Instead, we usually rotate villages throughout the region to reach the most people. During the trip, one of our nurses came to find me and brought me over to the line where people were waiting for care. The same young blind woman had lined up for care, too. I sat next to the translators so I could hear what she had to say. She proceeded to tell us that she had come to the medical team last year and that someone had prayed for her to receive her sight. She said that she was still blind when she left, but that she soon began to see in one of her eyes. She asked if we could again pray for her so that she could have more sight. Of course, we did! I have not seen her again but await a testimony in heaven of the Lord's healing grace on her.

Later that year, a few of us were delivering food to some elderly village residents who were sick and could not work. It had been a particularly dry year. The farmers' crop-yields were low as a result. There were many poor residents in this region, but the couple we were visiting that day was particularly poor because they had no strength to care for themselves nor did they have a family who could watch after them. Their neighbors would help them as they were able, but most everyone was struggling, so the help they could get was limited.

As we entered the elderly couple's small and humble home, we could see the only food that they had. They only had one bowl of potatoes to eat, and most of them were rotten. We had learned of this family while we were with some local farmers teaching them how to cultivate their crops more efficiently.

We visited with this elderly couple for a short time and left them with some large, fresh sacks of rice and flour. They were so grateful! As we were leaving the premises, we exited through a narrow walkway toward the dirt road. I was last in line. As we exited, I simply asked the Lord silently under my breath, "Bless this poor couple." I then petitioned, "Please visit them."

To my amazement, I heard a voice behind me in reply. I turned around quickly because I was unaware that anyone was following me. I thought I was last in line. When I turned around, no one was there. The voice had said, audibly, "I just did." This was the Lord's reply to my supplication to visit the people we had just encountered.

These types of examples have been significant to me in shaping how I view the work that we do for Him in the dark and unreached villages. These small acts of love and the testimonies we share are among the very few examples they see of Christ's presence and love. Yet we aren't doing work and asking the Lord to join. We are actually the ones joining Jesus in the work He is doing–because the work is His to begin with! If we grasp this truth, it gives us a great sense of humility, because we are able to see that in all that we do for Him, it is *He* who works for "His good pleasure" (see Philippians 2:13). Beyond that, He has chosen us (imperfect vessels) to carry His presence (see II Timothy 2:20-21). This is a sobering and very *real* truth.

When we felt God prompting us to begin the work in China, we took small steps forward without any clue concerning how it would grow. Most things we accomplish in the Kingdom of God are like that. We almost never know the result from the onset. In fact, the result is usually not what we had initially envisioned when we started.

If someone were to approach you in your teenage years and introduce you to someone you had not yet met, and told you that this new acquaintance was going to be your future life-long spouse, you, like most people, would likely be surprised. Indeed, it would probably be a shock! Of course, in some cultures, this is a common practice, but in western culture, it is not. If this arrangement took place, you might be pleasantly surprised and think, *Wow, I didn't expect that I would be so blessed!* or perhaps you would think, *Oh, that's not what I expected.* Either way, this news would be an important life-changing event, and for the rest of your premarriage life, you would shape your life based on your knowledge of what the future is holding for you.

Like with this illustration, if we knew our own futures, it certainly would change the way that we approach life and approach the Lord. Although it may satisfy our curiosity, it unfortunately would also deprive us of the beautiful experiences and struggles in taking steps of faith and trusting in Him alone. We would miss the reward of seeing how He unfolds the future before our eyes. This is how ministry develops. We don't know the future until it happens! And we don't know the full story until we can look back on it.

This way of living is so important in walking as a servant of the Lord. We must always walk in faith knowing that He holds our future. The steps He asks us to take will point us toward and bring us *into* His destiny for us. We may not know the end, but we do know the One who does, and that is enough for us. We each are born again with His seed and that is a seed of greatness. How that greatness will manifest is determined by our willingness to put trust in the One who is trustworthy.

I've experienced plenty of challenges as well as breakthroughs. I've walked through failures and hurts. My faith has been challenged and I've seen God move miraculously and show His love no matter how masked or how difficult things may have otherwise seemed. But, after all of these years, the thing that amazes me the most is that I'm always amazed when He comes through and demonstrates how much He is *for us* and how much He loves His people. Why does this still amaze me?

Servants & Spies is about the Lord. It's about His heart for others and His heart for you. It's a testimony of how He *can* and *will* come through when our hopes seem vague and our work for Him is difficult. It is about how your heart's yearning and dreaming for more of Him is not aimless or in vain. Rather, it's a desire He has planted within you to fulfill His call to establish His righteousness and His Kingdom in a place that only He can reach: *your heart.*

Your story may develop the same way mine did. It may unfold in a completely *different* manner. Regardless, my hope is that these stories and words will encourage you along the way and give you the heart-tips you need to enter into all that He has for you. In this, you will see yourself as His servant and His spy, sent from the Kingdom of Heaven to love and serve the people of your generation.

Where will your story begin? Or where *did* it begin? It must begin somewhere. For us, the Lord began His work in our hearts before we ever knew He called us to work with Him in China. And He began His work in China long before we ever went there. And certainly, He will continue His work long after we are gone. But where did all this begin for us?

I recall one event that helped to shape my understanding and clue me into the mystery He held for us. I was a young lawyer with an active practice with a large law firm in North Carolina. My wife and I were active in our local church and were attending regular Sunday school classes. I had served as the *president* of the Sunday school class—*the title was classy, but the role was merely administrative.*

During that time, there was a couple in our church who had

been preparing to serve in China on the mission field. This was in the early 1990s before China became as open to the West as it is now. We really didn't know this couple well, but we had known about their intentions to move to China as missionaries. We never took any particular interest in their plans. It seemed too far-fetched and certainly not something that we were interested in doing, as well. They were quite an odd couple anyhow, and it seemed particularly odd for them to have such a passion for a poor communist country on the other side of the globe. We even joked about them from time to time.

One day, they came to our Sunday School class to share about their plans to travel to China to begin their ministry. While we were waiting to hear them speak, I remember leaning over to nonchalantly whisper in my wife's ear, "Why would anyone want to go to China? That's the last place I'd want to go." Little did I know that His plans for our work in China had now begun!

The same types of things may be happening for you. Your work and destiny in the Lord has already begun, whether you know it or not. Perhaps the work ahead for you is something which you currently know nothing about. While He has already begun it, you simply don't see it yet. We should praise God for this! In fact, I encourage you to put this book down now and spend some time simply praising Him that He has a plan, that plan has begun, and His plan is even greater than you can imagine. Praise Him because this is true and because He is simply worthy of it!

The journey of making wise choices and steps of faith will determine how soon you can join the work He has already begun. But meanwhile, we must allow Him to prepare the ground in our own hearts to receive the seed of His vision, so we will grow spiritually and enter into our destinies well prepared.

The first and most important step in the journey of faith and serving God is to make sure that you have a personal relationship with Him. If you don't, then we need to take care of that now before you read on. Nothing else matters more. If we know Him, everything makes sense. If we don't, nothing makes sense, including the stories in this book.

You need to decide now if you wish to allow the Lord Jesus to be Lord of your life. This is a personal decision that you must make individually. This is the *only way* to eternal life with Him. We cannot just receive Him to be a part of our lives. We must ask Him to be Lord of all of it. He is ready, willing, and able to forgive you of all sin—yes, *all sin*!

He is waiting to rejoice in a relationship with you more than you will ever know. If you have not yet received Jesus as Lord of your life, please stop here and go to page 151 entitled *Prayer of Salvation.* Read it out loud prayerfully and ask the Lord Jesus to be your Savior and the Lord of your life from this day forward. Then, let's proceed with the journey.

2

A HEART'S DESIRE

"Deep calls unto deep at the noise of Your waterfalls; all Your waves and billows have gone over me." (Psalm 42:7)

"For it is God who works in you both to will and to do for His good pleasure." (Philippians 2:13)

"Delight yourself also in the LORD, And He shall give you the desires of your heart." (Psalm 37:4)

THE MUSIC WAS BEAUTIFUL. It strangely captured my emotions and my heart even more than it did my ears. I have always been what I consider a *thinker*, as one who evaluates situations and environments logically instead of emotionally. But that day, my emotions were vulnerable. I couldn't *think* well; I could only *feel*. It was one of those rare occasions when I could see with my emotions, and my ability to *think* through a process had to play catch-up. My brain was not in control—my heart was. I don't understand my emotions all that well, except in rare cases like this one. I know emotions are very real and I respect those who are in touch with theirs more regularly.

I had listened to my daughter, Joy, practice her piano many times before. It was always enjoyable, but it was usually just a routine for her that had become good background music in our home. The songs she played became very familiar and predictable —especially those places in each song that she was still working on and had not yet mastered.

She was a middle-school student at the time and was loving the process of learning the skill. Her grandfather (my dad) played piano and would play with her and encourage her in her musical development. They shared this as a mutual passion and it helped to bond them closer. My parents lived about four hours from us, so we did not see them too often, and those times we were together with them were special for us and for our four children. My father was quiet and reserved, but he loved to share those things he was particularly passionate about, including piano.

Joy especially liked the sound and the feel of my dad's grand piano. It was a Knabe piano that has a *jazz* sound, which was his favorite type of music, having grown up in the jazz era. Joy was not a fan of jazz music, but she certainly was a fan of playing piano with her grandfather. Those times were meaningful. The piano that we had in our own home at the time wasn't quite as nice as his grand piano. It could still make music even though it was so old that it could not be properly tuned. It was sufficient for Joy to develop her skill and follow her passion, until she eventually inherited her grandfather's piano after his death. It was certainly sufficient to grasp my emotions that day.

I had been working with our family's horses on that Saturday afternoon. It was a typical weekend, after a usual busy week of work at the office. Since it was hot outside, I came into the house for a break. As I lay on the sofa resting, listening to Joy practice her piano, I felt deep loneliness inside—and it wasn't the first time I had felt that. I had the incomplete sense that I was not where God wanted me to be and that I was disappointing Him and my family. I was so blessed to have such a wonderful life, with a wonderful family and career. We had four beautiful children, two boys and two girls, and they all knew the Lord. Yet, something deep inside my heart was very unsatisfied. It wasn't a disappointment brought on by not having what I wanted. It was a yearning that I couldn't identify. It was a sense that I knew there was more, and I wanted more; more of Him, more of His heart, yet I didn't know how to get from *here* to *there* because I was only *me.*

As I heard the music, and as I knew the lyrics all too well, I felt the pain of disappointment that I had no power to change myself, but only to watch Him from a distance. The distance between Him and me and His plan for my life seemed to be increasing. I felt I had drifted further and further away. I felt the opportunities lost, dreams unattained, and I was becoming what I had always vowed never to become—*normal.* Life isn't supposed to be that way; at least, it was not supposed to be that way for me. I felt very alone. I knew the Lord and I loved Him, but I felt so lost. I once again began to cry and hoped that no one would notice.

I remembered experiences from when I was a young child. I had an older brother and a younger sister. We grew up in a small town on Long Island, New York. I used to play alone in our family's playroom which was in the downstairs half of our split-level residence. I recalled that when I was alone and playing, I felt like someone was watching me. Sometimes it would feel a bit creepy (as a child's imagination often allows), but most of the time, it did not. I would sometimes look around to see who it was. I would look up toward the top of the stairs and felt someone was there overseeing what I was doing.

I sometimes even personified this sense and made this *overseer* into my *imaginary friend.* I even gave him a name. My friend seemed to be watching me, guarding me, and I knew I was safe. I didn't realize it then, but I think it was the eyes of the Lord and/or His angel there watching me and teaching me to be sensitive to Him and His presence. The Word tells us that "*The eyes of the Lord are in every place, beholding the good and the evil*" (Proverbs 15:3), and that, *"He shall give His angels charge over you, To keep you in all your ways"* (Psalm 91:11). He tells us that a child's angel is always, *"Beholding the face of [the] father who is in heaven"* (Matthew 18:10). I'm still not sure what it was during those years, but I am sure now that He has always been there.

Yet there I was, an adult, who had lost that sense. Had He left me? Had He become disappointed in me because I didn't amount to what He had hoped? Is this why the sense of His presence was gone? I pondered this in tears that afternoon on the sofa. *Lord, where are You?*

I was raised in a Christian home, but I didn't truly give my heart to the Lord until I was in high school. I had attended a Christian retreat during spring break of my tenth-grade year. The retreat was at a small farm in the mountains of the beautiful Shenandoah Valley. While I was there, the group began the meetings with worship songs. This was new to me. That weekend, I had the opportunity to watch others worship the Lord in a way I had never known. They clearly knew Him intimately, and I didn't—*but I wanted to.* Today, I still wonder if *anyone* could be in an environment of true worship like that and remain neutral. I think that a person will either be drawn into the worship and desire to know the Lord, or be repelled by it and run away because they are not yet willing to repent and embrace Him. I guess it all depends upon where your heart is. During that retreat, I received the Lord, and shortly afterward, I received His Holy Spirit. As an added bonus that weekend, I also met a wonderful and beautiful lady, Karen, who eventually would become my wife and ministry partner of 40 years!

I remember, as a young adult, how I loved the Lord. It was my heart's desire to serve Him. I knew that He had His hand on my life to serve Him and I knew that I needed to be prepared. I didn't want to waste any more time, so I left my university studies to take a leap of faith and transferred to Bible college to prepare for ministry. My hopes were that with these pursuits and preparations, He would count me worthy enough to enter into His service.

After finishing Bible college, my wife and I returned to our home state of Virginia to serve the youth of our church and begin our family. At that time, we had a healthy young daughter and another one on the way. The evangelist who had led me to the Lord was beginning a new church in the Shenandoah Valley of Virginia and He asked me to come and lead the youth. We answered his request and joined him in ministry. It was a position of volunteer ministry, so I worked full-time at the local hospital to support us as we served in the church.

Our ministry grew. In fact, after a few months, we had more youth attending our meetings than we had members of the church. God's heart was clearly moving among the young people of the land and His destiny was on them to be a light to their peers. It was an exciting time. I was proud of our youth. As I reveled in the strength of our youth and the ministry, I began to allow pride and criticism enter my heart. I shared with our pastor that our youth group was strong and in a place that would take most churches years to achieve. He kindly but quickly reminded me with a subtle but well-taken message, "It did." I gulped. He was right. The youth were children of the mature believers in the church, and they had been trained and discipled by their parents, not me. It was a good lesson.

After running the youth ministry for several years, I felt the Lord was bringing change in our lives and wanted to broaden our foundation as a family. It was quite challenging for me to work in the ministry while also working a full-time secular job and raising a family. I didn't know which direction to go. I had hopes, but I didn't see how I could do it.

I took some time off from work and from the ministry, and I went up into the mountains to fast and pray. I packed my tent and clothes, then drove to the George Washington National Forest. I parked my car in a convenient clearing at the top of the mountains and I hiked until I found a clearing where I could see down the mountain, set up my tent, and spend some time with the Lord.

I fasted. I sought the Lord for His plan. I prayed, "Lord, it is my heart's desire to serve You!" But inside, I felt that He was bringing an end to this chapter in our lives and that He was bringing us to a new place. I said, "Lord, You have given me Your vision for the youth of the church, but now You want to end it?" I wondered, *What should I do?*

As I was still in the mountains praying, I wrote out what I believed was God's vision and plan on a piece of paper. I dug a hole in the ground under a rock and I buried the paper. I told the Lord it was my heart's desire to serve Him, but I knew there was a change coming. I asked the Lord that when it was time to resurrect His vision, in His time, and in His power, that He would do it. But for the time being, I simply left it in His hands. I departed from the mountain and returned to my home and family.

Later in life, I pondered what I did by burying that paper under the rock. It dawned on me that I may have *buried my talent* as Jesus spoke of in Matthew 25:14-30, when the wicked servant buried His talent in the ground instead of investing it. I realized later that this is not what happened. I didn't bury His talent, but merely needed to come to an end of what I could do myself–even in ministry. This was part of His next step for us.

Maybe it is your heart's desire to serve the Lord, like it was mine; and maybe there are things that you have been doing to serve Him, even very successful things. But the Lord will sometimes bring us to the point that we must lay down what we are doing in order to come into a new place and season. Sometimes the pathway to the new season is not so direct, but as we will see, He is always faithful to direct us, and He will always be at work to fulfill His call on our lives.

After the mountain-top burial, I returned to the university and later attended law school so that I could better provide for my family. As I laid there on the sofa that day, reflecting on all of this, ministry and mission work seemed like a lifetime away. I was now a practicing health care lawyer and ministry prospects seemed to be becoming distant more and more each day. I felt that maybe I had left the Lord's plan—like I had failed Him, and inside, I just grieved.

As I listened to my daughter playing worship songs on the piano and loving the Lord with all of her heart, my heart yearned to be like her. I hungered for that experience, too. Recently, both of my daughters had joined mission trips while they were in middle school, and in fact, my youngest daughter, Lynn, still travels frequently and ministers prophetically in more countries than I have ever been to. I was, and am, so proud of both of them.

As I lay there listening, I said in my heart, "Lord, I would love to go on a mission trip someday... but I am too old." I would be turning 40 later that year and realized how many opportunities I had missed to complete the call I had always felt in my heart. I knew that was not a good place for me to be. I had thought that mission work was only for the young generation and that I had missed it.

I also recalled my favorite uncle, who had a deep influence on my coming to Christ. My father was a godly man. He was also a fraternal twin. His twin sister, my Aunt Betty, had become a missionary in Africa. She had met her husband, Uncle Don, while on the mission field and they married. When I was a child, we didn't get to see them very often because they lived in Africa most of the time and only came home for short visits every few years. Uncle Don loved us kids. I could sense his love for us. I idolized him and craved his attention. He often spent hours with us playing card games. I remember so enjoying the game of Rook, yet we only played it when he was visiting.

The most common phrase I would hear my uncle say was, "Praise the Lord." This was odd to me because I had never heard anyone proclaim that before. But he said it often; not just after hearing a nice testimony or as part of a conversation, but he would say it even when he was alone. He loved Jesus and he let Jesus know this continually. I knew that he was a special man sent by God.

I mention Uncle Don because he told me something personal one time that changed my life forever. I will never forget it and I share it with others as often as I can. It came to mind that afternoon while lying on the sofa listening to Joy play piano.

Uncle Don got very serious and said that he had something very important for me to know. I was in high school at the time. He said to me, "There are only two things in life that last forever: *the Word of God* and *people.*" He said, "If we invest our lives into these two things, our work will last forever." I thought, *Wow, that is true.* God's Word is eternal and existed at the very beginning of time. John 1:1 tells us that: *"In the beginning was the Word, and the Word was with God, and the Word was God."* And it is true that the soul of a person will last forever–eternally, either in hell or in heaven with the Lord.

So, I thought, *this means that if we invest ourselves, our lives, our time, and our resources into the Word of God and into people, then our investment will remain forever, too.* That seemed like a good deal to me and a much better investment than stocks or even gold!

I wanted to do this badly. I did love the Word. But that afternoon, I felt so far from that and did not know if I would ever be able to serve like Uncle Don did and see the eternal result of my work on earth. We will spend a lot of time in eternity, and it sure would be nice if our work on earth would have an eternal impact. After all, eternity has already begun, but it seemed like the progress, or *lack of progress* in my life had stalled it.

The *indirect* route I traveled to ministry was not a wrong path. It never changed my desire to serve Him and it never changed His purpose. Instead, it was my understanding that was not correct. I didn't see or understand how God was at work within me to bring me to the place where He actually could use me in the work He destined for me. God needed to change my heart to prepare me for what He had in mind for us ahead. I needed to sense that I was not where He wanted me to be, so that I would reach out to Him to prepare me because I could not prepare myself. I needed to feel the sense that somehow I had come up short and that it seemed impossible to ever return and to do what He created me to do.

But, what I had viewed as a *negative* thing, i.e. the despair of feeling left behind and unable to move forward, was actually a gift. It was a gift because it spurred me on to getting serious with the Lord, and it helped me because I could not otherwise help myself. I was not ready for ministry, and I had no idea at that point if I ever would be. All I knew was that if there was any way to get from *here* to *there,* it would take a miracle of the Lord and only He could do that. I could not. I needed to see that I failed and would continue to fail if I relied on my own strength and abilities to do His work.

If I had not gone through this personal despair, I would not have reached out to the Lord for His supernatural hand. In that case, any attempt on my own to reach His destiny for my life (or even worse, entering ministry on my own without His enabling) would have been a disaster for me and my family. Ministry is not a light thing. It is deeply spiritual and impacts people, the church, and even nations. Even the smallest acts of ministry can be hugely impactful. We must be ready. At that point, I was not. Only He could make necessary changes.

As I was able to see my own inability to achieve what He and I both desired, I didn't realize that the process had already begun. It was His process of preparing and enabling me; His process of calling and commissioning us. He was changing my heart by taking from within me the "heart of stone" and replacing it with His "heart of flesh" (see Ezekiel 36:26). This was part of it, and I didn't know it. My deepest inner despair was the yearning of my heart's desire to have His heart, so He could launch what He had already instilled in my heart to do from the beginning! As I lay there on the couch, I gave him permission to do that. I just didn't know how it would happen.

For years, my daughter had no idea how her beautiful worship music began to break up the ground of my heart, which initiated the launch of a new lifestyle and ministry that ultimately would bring salvation and healing among nations. I had not openly shared this because it had been a painful part of my past. I had not wanted people to know or understand my inner struggle of my own sense of inadequacy to do what we do in ministry today. I have since come to understand that this is a *positive* aspect of the story. It is a story of His restoration and redemption, like only He can do. Yet it is not an isolated incident. He *can* and *will* do it for you also.

If you feel like this sometimes, I encourage you not to give up. Don't look inward at failures and disappointments, and certainly don't enter the death-spiral of thinking that it is too late to fulfill His perfect destiny for your life. It's not too late. I encourage you to do the very simple thing I did that afternoon: *turn to the Lord and simply tell Him how you feel.* Verbally give Him permission to change your heart and to do whatever He must do in your life to bring you into your destiny. Tell Him that you realize there are areas of your heart that may be hardened over that you cannot see. Tell Him you will trust Him to break up the hardened ground of your heart and prepare you for what is to come. His work in you has *already begun.*

3

HEAR HIM CALL. WHAT IS OUR ANSWER?

"Sow for yourselves righteousness; reap steadfast love; break up your fallow ground, for it is the time to seek the LORD, that he may come and rain." (Hosea 10:12)

"Keep your heart with all diligence, For out of it spring the issues of life." (Proverbs 4:23)

"Today, if you will hear His voice, Do not harden your hearts as in the rebellion." (Hebrews 3:15)

I AM ESPECIALLY BLESSED that all four of my children love and serve the Lord. I realize that this is a rare treasure and I wouldn't trade it for anything, *ever*. One thing that my children would tell you is that they feel part of their training for serving the Lord was in our family never finding roots in one single place. We were always flexible to flow into whatever was next. In fact, we actually moved homes nine times in a five-year period! I don't look back at that as positively as my kids do—but I am glad they see it that way.

One of the homes we lived in for 18 years was a home we built ourselves. To build the home, we served as the *general contractor* for the project, and we hired individual subcontractors to build their respective parts. For example, we had a foundation company pour concrete and brick-up the foundation. We then hired framers to build up the skeleton structure. We hired electricians, plumbers, carpenters, and so forth.

One of the most crucial parts of the building process was laying a proper foundation. We had to mark off the boundary as to how the house would be situated on the land as well as determine the home's exact dimensions and footprint. Once we did this, in order to begin the foundation, we had to *break ground.* If we were to do this with hand shovels, we would be working on that *still today*. It took professional equipment and professional equipment operators because the ground was hard and they needed to dig deep. Once the ground preparation was done, only then could the foundation be laid.

Of course, for ministry, it is *vitally* important to lay a firm foundation via faith in Christ and our understanding of our mission. Yet, we cannot even do that until the ground of our own hearts is prepared. We, personally, have a very important role to play in preparing our own hearts. Neglecting the preparation of our own hearts will result in a weak and shallow foundation. At times, preparing our own hearts is difficult because *plowing* the hard ground of our hearts can be painful. Hard ground takes work to break up. Yet in the end, it becomes pliable and useful, and it can hold the correct shape for the *house of His glory*–which is your ministry.

THE CALL OF ISAIAH

I had always pondered and wished for God to call me in a similar fashion to what we see in the sixth chapter of Isaiah. Let me explain: the prophet Isaiah saw the Lord on His throne and received a very dramatic invitation from the Lord to serve Him in a specific way. In the encounter, he was commissioned by the Lord to "go."

Isaiah was a well-known and well-respected prophet and the people of Israel put a lot of stock in what Isaiah would say. When the Lord spoke to Isaiah, He spoke both in visions and in words. Sometimes when we hear from the Lord, it may be difficult to know exactly how you are hearing because His words permeate our soul so deeply that sometimes the mode of communication is not clear to us. *Was that audible, visionary, or a deep voice in my spirit?* At times, we ask this, perplexed at the method. Have you ever experienced this? If not, ask the Lord and wait for His timing. He will do it! This has happened to me a few times, yet for the most part, the Lord will speak to us softly. Without question, He speaks to us, perhaps most consistently, through the reading of His Word.

The context of this encounter in Isaiah 6 is necessary to capture the full scope of what was happening. Israel's trusted leader, King Uzziah, had just died. The people of Israel had a long-placed trust in King Uzziah and his armies. They knew that he would protect them so that Israel could maintain their peace and prosperity amidst many outside threats. The problem was, *Uzziah died.* Israel became fearful and sensed that their security had just been compromised. They were uncertain of what would happen next. In the midst of their insecurity, the Lord then spoke to His prophet Isaiah:

> "In the year that King Uzziah died, I saw the Lord seated on a throne, high and exalted; and the train of His robe filled the temple. Above Him stood seraphim, each having six wings: With two wings they covered their faces, with two they covered their feet, and with two they were flying. And they were calling out to one another: 'Holy, holy, holy is the LORD of Hosts; all the earth

is full of His glory.' At the sound of their voices the doorposts and thresholds shook, and the temple was filled with smoke.

"Then I said: 'Woe is me, for I am ruined, because I am a man of unclean lips dwelling among a people of unclean lips; for my eyes have seen the King, the LORD of Hosts.' Then one of the seraphim flew to me, and in his hand was a glowing coal that he had taken with tongs from the altar. And with it he touched my mouth and said: 'Now that this has touched your lips, your iniquity is removed and your sin is atoned for.' Then I heard the voice of the Lord saying: 'Whom shall I send? Who will go for Us?' And I said: 'Here am I. Send me!'" (Isaiah 6:1-8)

One of the most compelling parts of this experience is that Isaiah heard the Lord's question, "Whom shall I send?" Isaiah loved the Lord and desired to please Him, so he answered, "Here I am, send me." God *wanted* someone to send and Isaiah *wanted* to be sent.

This tells us that the Lord was asking this question throughout heaven, which was the place He brought Isaiah to hear His voice. He was inquiring, "Whom shall I send?" I believe He is *still* asking that question *even now.* Sometimes we may hear it—sometimes we may *not* hear it. Yet, either way, His purposes have not changed since Isaiah's time. God wishes to show His glory to all the earth, and He desires to send His children to make it happen. Do we wish to be a part of this? Do we long to be sent? Have we answered the Lord and said, "Here I am, send me"? Consider this call and consider how you will *answer* the call. Contemplate how you may position yourself so that you can, indeed, be sent.

The Lord would prefer to send those who wish to be sent, but not everyone is willing. Jonah is perhaps the seminal example of one who was unwilling. In the end, after much difficulty, he became willing.

Today, if we hear His voice, we *must* answer. This is so important in order for our Gospel message to go forward. Even Jesus asked us to pray that God would send laborers into the harvest (see Luke 10:2). You may not physically hear and experience His call like Isaiah did, but even today He is calling throughout heaven and He awaits our answer. I pray that we will all hear His voice asking who He could send, and that the voice of a multitude will answer with a willing heart by saying, “Here I am, send me.” If we do this, the Lord will answer us and send us, but we have to prepare our hearts accordingly.

You might be wondering, *Where am I agreeing to go? What am I agreeing to do?* The answer: *wherever He sends you and whatever He sends you to do.* Answering the call is not about knowing all of the methods and means immediately. The call could be down the street or around the world. The call could be to continue influencing people at your nine-to-five or to drop everything to live in a mud hut in Africa. When we say *yes,* the rest unfolds thereafter. When the Lord asks us to *go*, He will send us accordingly. Yet, there is certainly a time of preparation that is necessary. We need to see more clearly *where* He is asking us to go and *what* He is asking us to do. This is part of the process of preparing our own hearts. The Lord will prepare us and test us before He will send us.

For Isaiah, the Lord took the next necessary steps to help prepare him. Symbolically, the Lord had to cleanse Isaiah by touching his lips with a burning coal. This suggested a cleansing of Isaiah’s flesh by the holy fire of God and an imparting of God’s words to Isaiah so that he would declare the words he was being sent to declare. This reflects the very important stages of preparation of our lives before we launch into what God has called us to do. Allow His holy fire to cleanse your way so that you may have a pure heart to serve Him. Without fail, He will continue to do this throughout our entire lives.

THE DOUBLE PORTION ANOINTING

For years, I pondered the *double portion* anointing of Elijah when I came across it in Scripture. I even longed for it. Elijah was the most known and respected prophet of the Lord. He was known for many great miracles and exploits, including the heroic showdown on Mount Carmel where he faced-off against the prophets of Baal who had been enlisted by Ahab and Jezebel (see 1 Kings 18). Elijah triumphed, slew the prophets of Baal, and later defeated Jezebel and Ahab. He was known and feared as a man of God. Elisha had been the servant of Elijah. He was his disciple and learned from Elijah as he faithfully served him for three-and-a-half years.

In 2 Kings, Elijah was coming close to the end of his ministry. He asked Elisha three different times to stay and wait for him while he traveled off to take care of some business, as he had likely done many times before. Elisha may have known that his time with Elijah would soon be coming to a close, so he expressed to Elijah that he wanted to be permitted to come with him.

> "And it came to pass, when the Lord was about to take up Elijah into heaven by a whirlwind, that Elijah went with Elisha from Gilgal. Then Elijah said to Elisha, 'Stay here, please, for the Lord has sent me on to Bethel.' But Elisha said, 'As the Lord lives, and as your soul lives, I will not leave you!' So they went down to Bethel. Now the sons of the prophets who were at Bethel came out to Elisha, and said to him, 'Do you know that the Lord will take away your master from over you today?' And he said, 'Yes, I know; keep silent!'
>
> "Then Elijah said to him, 'Elisha, stay here, please, for the Lord has sent me on to Jericho.' But he said, 'As the Lord lives, and as your soul lives, I will not leave you!' So they came to Jericho. Now the sons of the prophets who were at Jericho came to Elisha and said to him, 'Do you know that the Lord will take

away your master from over you today?' So he answered, 'Yes, I know; keep silent!' Then Elijah said to him, 'Stay here, please, for the Lord has sent me on to the Jordan.'

"But he said, 'As the Lord lives, and as your soul lives, I will not leave you!' So the two of them went on. And fifty men of the sons of the prophets went and stood facing them at a distance, while the two of them stood by the Jordan. Now Elijah took his mantle, rolled it up, and struck the water; and it was divided this way and that, so that the two of them crossed over on dry ground. And so it was, when they had crossed over, that Elijah said to Elisha, 'Ask! What may I do for you, before I am taken away from you?' Elisha said, 'Please let a double portion of your spirit be upon me.'

"So he said, 'You have asked a hard thing. Nevertheless, if you see me when I am taken from you, it shall be so for you; but if not, it shall not be so.' Then it happened, as they continued on and talked, that suddenly a chariot of fire appeared with horses of fire, and separated the two of them; and Elijah went up by a whirlwind into heaven. And Elisha saw it, and he cried out, 'My father, my father, the chariot of Israel and its horsemen!' So he saw him no more. And he took hold of his own clothes and tore them into two pieces. He also took up the mantle of Elijah that had fallen from him, and went back and stood by the bank of the Jordan. Then he took the mantle of Elijah that had fallen from him, and struck the water, and said, 'Where is the Lord God of Elijah?' And when he also had struck the water, it was divided this way and that; and Elisha crossed over." (2 Kings 2:1-14)

Elijah also must have known that his ministry time was soon ending and that Elisha wished to succeed him. I believe this is why he tested Elisha three times to see if he would *go the distance.* This reminds me of the three opportunities Jesus gave Peter to either acknowledge Him or deny Him before His crucifixion. Later, after

His resurrection, Christ offered redemption to Peter when He asked him three times if Peter loved Him (see Luke 22:54-62). So, for Elisha, there was a period of testing, and he passed. He remained faithful to his master even though the sad departure was soon to occur.

To me, it is compelling that Elisha's last request to his master Elijah was that he would not just receive his anointing and serve as his successor, but that he would receive a "double potion." Elisha was *all in.*

I've asked the Lord many times for a *double portion.* I have never been sure what that would look like or what it indeed would be as applied to the ministry He called me to carry out. Nonetheless, I wanted it in *double.* As Elijah told Elisha, "You ask a hard thing." The Holy Spirit has asked me also if I really wanted this and if I would be willing to go through with it. I have always answered in the affirmative.

As I look back over the years and at the experiences I've had, I can understand what Elijah meant by suggesting that such a request is a "hard thing." It's not a hard thing to ask for and it's not a hard thing for the Lord to grant. But it *is* a hard thing for us to walk through. His call is so compelling that we know that He wants us to push forward, but at times, the life circumstances and opposition are so compellingly difficult that it's not easy to determine if we made the right decision or not. Yet, it *is* all worth it.

As I've observed, there is usually a break-in-time between when we sense or hear the Lord's call on our life and the time He actually commissions us to go. For Isaiah, it seems to have been just a moment, but that moment included this holy impartation and cleaning. For Elisha, it was a longer daily walk of serving his master for years. Usually, the Lord will let us know His call, and then, like we see with Elisha's example, there is a period of testing and preparation.

Please do not discount the necessary steps of preparation and commissioning before launching into ministry. As instructed by Paul, servants of the Lord must be ready, "In season and out of season" (see II Timothy 4:2). Ministry is not a task—it is warfare. You must be equipped and trained like any modern-day soldier in a country's army. Our weapons are spiritual and we must learn when and how to use them effectively (see II Corinthians 10:4-6). If a soldier were to learn to shoot a weapon without learning how to aim it properly, what good is that training? Don't discount and discredit the preparatory training. Don't become impatient with it. Remember, Jesus didn't start His ministry until He was 30. We are not better than Him nor should we jump the gun. God is not in a hurry; He would much rather build a laborer who lasts than a laborer who caves quickly.

Our hearts must be ready to receive His call and even more ready to walk in it. Today, you too may ask the Lord for an Isaiah 6 experience. Or perhaps if you have received His call, you may ask Him for an Elisha experience to receive a *double portion* of His anointing (however that may look). But the most important things are for you to be patient and allow Him to prepare your own heart and wait for the time that He will ask you to begin.

4

BUILDING AND SHAPING: AN INSTANTANEOUS AND A LIFE-LONG PROCESS

> "One day is as a thousand years, and a thousand years as one day." (I Peter 3:8)

> "But Jesus answered them, 'My Father has been working until now, and I have been working.'" (John 5:17)

WE HAD BEEN LIVING in a rental home temporarily while we became familiar with the new city where we had just moved. At that time, I was working for a medium-sized law firm in Richmond, Virginia, but had been given the responsibility to start a satellite office in Raleigh, North Carolina. We moved to a rental home in the rural areas south of Raleigh, in order to save money to purchase a home once we had learned the housing market. We had hoped to find a home where we could have our horses on our own land, but land was expensive. As an alternative, we hoped to find a home where we could stable our horses at a community pasture nearby.

Our family loved horses, though we had not owned them for very long. My daughters loved to ride. I enjoyed riding, too, and it was actually my idea to have horses to begin with. They weren't show-quality, but anyone familiar with the industry knows that even inexpensive horses can be remarkably expensive to raise. A friend once said to me, "Owning horses was like buying a hole in the ground that you throw money into." I think he was right.

My daughters each had their own horse. Sometimes they would ride them together and play "tag" with each other. They would ride bare-back (meaning they would ride without a proper saddle) and by touching their opponent's horse with their foot, they would tag them as "it." I didn't learn of this until later–I would have been horrified had I known it earlier because horses can be as unpredictably dangerous as they are beautiful and fun. We learned that lesson a few years later when my wife was thrown off of my favorite horse (whom I had named *Rolex* because he was beautiful and strong). She suffered a concussion and had to get her leg bones reattached surgically. We didn't keep Rolex much longer.

We finally purchased a home in a horse-friendly neighborhood in Raleigh and moved in. We housed the horses on-site at our home until space opened up at the neighborhood stalls and we were able to move them to the better accommodations. We began settling into our home and new life in Raleigh. We soon learned that we had stretched ourselves financially more than we should have and we needed to find a way back to a proper budget. Although we had hoped to be in a position of strength for future ministry, we didn't think we were in a position to do that quite yet. We figured it would take a lot of time before we could reach out to others when we ourselves had need.

One evening at our church home group, the leader felt prompted by the Lord that some of us in the group had some unmet financial needs. He said he felt led to ask all of us to put our wallets into the center of the room. We then gathered around them in a circle and prayed that the Lord would fill them supernaturally. I thought it was a bit funny, but nonetheless, we know that God is amazingly creative. By no coincidence, the next week, we got our answer. So too did most of the home group! It was exciting and unusual. For us, we didn't know it was the answer at the time, but it was... one night, *our house burned down!*

THE FIRE

I had come home from work and was reading the newspaper. My wife, Karen, came to me and said that it might be good for me to check the attic. She had just been up there to store some of our children's toys. She said that she smelled smoke and her eyes burned, so there may be a leak in the fireplace flue. It wouldn't have been unthinkable, given that we had been burning wood in the free-standing wood stove.

When I went up to the attic, I saw smoke rising from the area where the flue came through the attic floor. I pulled back the insulation and saw that our house was on fire. We quickly got our children out of the house and called 911. We moved our cars out of the driveway so the fire department could access the house. By that time, the flames were growing and everyone in the neighborhood knew that the house was on fire. A crowd emerged and our neighbors were nervous about whether their homes would be affected also.

The house was almost a total loss. Most of the ground floor was still in place, but the upstairs and attic were gone. Fortunately, we were all okay! We spent the next few nights in a hotel until we could rent a house nearby.

We felt up-rooted again and didn't know *how* or *when* we could move forward. Since most of our personal belongings were destroyed, we had to once again rebuild our lives. Why did this happen? Why did we have to once again come to an end of who we were and what we had built? We had a family... yet we had to restart our lives *again?*

We could have stayed discouraged, but to be honest, it was hard to do so. We knew the Lord. We knew that He was in this situation and that He was building our lives for His next step for us. In fact, our family joined together to work through this and it made us stronger. Others joined around us to help also.

I was particularly touched when, during the first week after the fire, our son's school class took up an offering of clothing and other personal items to share with our kids. It was beautiful to see that others cared for us and reached out to us, even though it was our desire to reach out to them.

Sometimes receiving help is humbling. I think as people who are called as servants of the Lord, we must learn to receive, too. We must know what it is like to have need and to be on the "receiving-end" of the need before we can truly understand the perspective of those we will reach out to in our lives.

Losing our home and all of our belongings seemed like a negative experience—but it wasn't. The Lord had to once again tear down elements of the fleshly structure we created in our hearts by tearing down the physical one that we relied on. He did this so He could build the kingdom of God in our hearts to prepare us for the next step, even though it seemed to be a delay. What looked to us like a step backwards was actually necessary so that our feet could move forward in the new direction He wanted us to walk.

We spent the next year searching for and purchasing land in the rural countryside outside of the city of Raleigh. We decided to build our own home. We hired subcontractors to handle building certain aspects of the home, but some of it we built ourselves. This enabled us to save money and also to work together on a family project. I even remember my young daughter, Lynn, helping to put siding and shingles on the home. It seemed like a nice idea, but as time went on, we definitely wished we had hired someone to build it for us entirely. Yet, by making this a family project, we were able to purchase more space that gave us room for expansion for our ministry and that freed us up financially to make other decisions.

During this season of life, we attended a home group meeting regularly. After one particular meeting, we were in the kitchen snacking when the host approached me and asked me a question I never thought I would hear. He said, "Would you like to come with us on a mission trip?" *A mission trip?* I thought. I didn't think that was possible, and even if it was possible, it didn't seem reasonable. After all, I was almost 40 years old! I thought that I was certainly too old. Additionally, I remembered that we were recovering from a complete upheaval in our housing. A mission trip didn't seem smart. I thought about it for a short moment, and after talking about it with Karen, I decided to take the risk of looking and feeling foolish, and I said, "Yes, I will go."

The plans for the mission trip had already begun. When I joined the team, I saw there were others on the team who were my age, as well—this was encouraging to me. I did feel a little out of place, but I knew it was the Lord's plan. So now, my heart asked, "Why am I going and what will He do?" I didn't know for sure, but I had my secret hopes.

As we prepared for the trip, I wanted so badly for it to be an intimate time with the Lord that would change my life forever. As the song goes, I wanted Him to, "Break my heart for what breaks His." I wanted to feel His heartbeat. I wanted Him to change me. I wanted Him to bring His destiny in our lives. I have to admit I was nervous because I thought, *What if He doesn't do these things? What if this is in vain and I just wasted our family resources on a personal trip?* Nevertheless, I just trusted Him and decided to act. As a result, that summer of 2001, I went to Kazakhstan.

What was the grand project I was to accomplish in Kazakhstan? What did I, as an American lawyer, have to offer the Kazak people that would brilliantly explain what they did not have? How were my gifts and talents to be used on this exciting mission trip? I pondered these things. Each team member had specific jobs. Some worked on the construction of housing for an addiction recovery center. Others worked on teaching computers to local villagers. My task? I dug a hole with a shovel for a new latrine at the orphanage.

I came to Kazakhstan to dig a hole?! I could have paid the trip money to a local man to dig the hole instead, right? Why did I come all the way to the other part of the world to dig a hole? How would this change my heart and change the world? Although I didn't have the answer to these questions, I decided it was best to proceed with my job, to give 110% of my effort, and to dig the best hole for the best latrine that these kids could have. After all, if they had to use an outdoor latrine, as orphan children, they deserved a good one. So, I dug.

As I dug up the ground for the latrine, the Lord was preparing ground in my own heart. How could He plant seeds of faith for my future if my own heart was not fully pliable? How unique was this project that it was seemingly a prophetic act of my digging the ground to serve others, while He was digging the ground of my heart so that I could have a strong foundation to serve even more!

We dug... *and we dug.* We built... *and we built.* The latrine was almost finished before we had to leave. Thankfully, I was able to return the next year to see the final result once it was all finished. It didn't seem to matter, though, because the true digging was in my heart.

While I was in Kazakhstan, during the early morning hours, I would venture to the backyard of the place we stayed so I could pray and prepare for the day ahead. During these times, I reflected on the people we had met the day before and the conditions they lived in. I considered what their needs were, how different they and their lifestyles were from mine, and how different they were inside. They were not selfish.

For some strange reason, each morning when I went out to pray, I wept. This time, however, I wasn't weeping for myself and my hope to change. Instead, it was a weeping for them, that the Lord would change life for them. I asked the Lord, "How can I help?" I made myself available for Him to use me in any way. So, by the end of the trip, I was quite excited to return to the project once again to dig.

Do we truly know what breaks the heart of God? Do we truly know how He sees us, how He sees others, and how He wants to use us? I think we see in part, but we never see the whole picture. When I returned to the USA, I was touched by the Lord and felt re-directed by Him. I was excited for this new heart He had given me for orphans and for the lost. I proceeded to study His Word and set out to understand the true nature of His heart for orphans and the poor.

I began a personal study that changed my life. It was a simple one. I looked up every verse in the Bible that mentioned "orphans" and the "fatherless." I then wrote out each verse and I categorized each verse based upon the message it gave about God's heart toward them. After finishing this, I stood back and was amazed. *Wow, the Lord has such a special status in His heart for orphans,* I thought.

I had no idea how personally the Lord looks at orphans, and at those who chose either to bless them or to do them harm! He makes provision for them and tenderly watches over them. He looks at them as their father. He identifies so closely with them that the Lord Himself even avenges Himself of His anger on those who purposefully abuse them (see Jeremiah 5:28-29). He gives them special status! So, I thought, *If we serve those whom You love so deeply, certainly it is pleasing to You.*

Our ministry has been varied throughout Russia, China, North Korea, and Kazakhstan. In all these areas, one of the fundamental roots has been His call to serve the orphans, widows, and those who cannot help themselves. Whenever we bless them, I can somehow feel the pleasure of the Lord. He loves them and He lets us know that. I have never had a natural inclination to be drawn to children. Yet, after allowing the Lord to plow the ground of my heart, He replaced it with His. He has given me His love for children.

One of my favorite books in the Bible is the book of Psalms. The Psalms reflect God's heart for us and ours for Him. I especially like Psalm 127:1 which was a song by Solomon teaching us that, *"Unless the Lord build the house, they that build it labor in vain."* Correspondingly, it says that, *"Unless the Lord guards the city, the watchman stays awake in vain."*

Our ministries are like a building structure. We labor and work to build the framework for the tasks He has called us to, and the Lord works and labors to build the framework in our hearts so that our labor is not in vain. The work is His, so we need to work together *with* Him, not merely *for* Him in this process.

As I was building our home, as I mentioned, there were times I wished I had not decided to build it ourselves. I imagine that the Lord sees us sometimes working to build our own ministries without allowing Him to do it by first building His kingdom in our hearts. Psalm 127 doesn't say that we will not have to labor in His work. It just tells us that the Lord must be the builder. We are His crew. But we must build what He has set for us and must do it with His proper oversight and involvement. Otherwise, it will be in vain, and at the end of the age, we may risk not hearing His pleasure (see Matthew 25:21).

None of us will live forever on this earth. Our time is set. The Lord knows the time of our birth and the appointed time of our death (see Ecclesiastes 3:1; Hebrews 9:27). At the conclusion of this life, we must all stand before the Judgment seat of Christ (see II Corinthians 5:10). If this wasn't true, He wouldn't have told us it was! It's a sobering future event that many of us believe will happen, but we like to put in the back of our minds because it is otherwise too difficult for us to contemplate daily. In fact, in Proverbs 21:12, the Lord tells us we need to number our own days. He says, "*Teach us to number our days aright, that we may gain a heart of wisdom.*"

Do we ever think about this? Do we ever envision whether the Lord will tell us, "Well done," or perhaps if He may have other words? This is important to think about because everything in our lives will be looked at and evaluated by the Lord. If He alone is the creator and master of time, how long do you think He will spend with us reviewing those details of our lives, and to what level of detail? I don't know, but *I do know* that with the Lord, *"One day is as a thousand years, and a thousand years as one day"* (I Peter 3:8). So, we should all consider what this may mean for us personally when the day comes that our lives are reviewed by the Lord in the context of *eternity*.

Matthew 25:13 tells us that if we are faithful in the things He has asked us to do, He will reply to us, *"Well done, thou good and faithful servant."* For those who were not faithful in the things He had asked them to do, the Lord's response will be much more severe. Do we long to hear our Lord say to us, "Well done"? I fear that the American church (and perhaps global church) has lost a sense of the fear of the Lord. We must all stand before Him on that day. Should we not fear Him now and assure that His response to us is a good one? If you are not sure, then this is the time to ask His Holy Spirit to look at your heart and search it. To replace any false way with His everlasting way so that on Judgement Day, you may hear Him say, "Well done!" (Psalm 139:23-24).

Allow the Lord to shape your heart. In doing so, He will also shape your ministry. To attempt to shape a ministry by bypassing the shaping of the heart is to ignore God's order of operations. Sometimes, the shaping of the heart may take longer than we wish. Good things take time to build. Yet, time is not as important as the actual process of Him changing us. In particular, pay close attention to what He is doing or asking you to do for those who are less fortunate than you are. He holds special status for orphans, widows, strangers, and the poor. God cares for the poor! When we care for them, we are working with Him.

Allow Him to show you areas in your life He may not be pleased with. This is healthy! It's part of His developing His character in us to be like Him, to be usable to Him, and to move us closer in obedience. In doing so, when we stand before His throne, there will be no surprises but only sweet fellowship and the revelation that the One who called us is pleased with our decisions and our work.

PART II

5

HE DOES HAVE A PLAN... AND SO SHOULD WE

> "Write the vision And make it plain on tablets, That he may run who reads it." (Habakkuk 2:2)

> "Being confident of this very thing, that He who has begun a good work in you will complete it until the day of Jesus Christ." (Philippians 1:6)

THE LORD STARTED our ministry in a different way than I expected. As we've discussed, He is always at work to prepare our hearts for Him to use us, and He has always been at work in our lives even before we knew it. Somehow, I'm always surprised at the fact that I'm surprised when I see His hand at work in our lives.

He is always at work on our behalf and to accomplish His purposes. It is up to us to allow Him to do His work in us, and it is up to us to respond with our actions when He does. We must remind ourselves that He is always at work, not just at the beginning, but *always*. No matter the circumstances or lack of circumstances, He will complete what He has begun. He doesn't drop it or change His mind in the middle. He does have a plan! We don't have to worry about whether it is a good plan or one that we don't like, because it *is* a good plan and it is designed specifically for us. We just need to situate ourselves to make sure we respond to Him and flow into it.

Our work in Kazakhstan set the stage for how we would see God move and how He would build this ministry over the next twenty years. During this time, we learned to listen, learned to watch, and learned to act. When we did, the Lord never failed to show Himself strong.

Second Chronicles 16:9 tells us that *"The eyes of the LORD run to and fro throughout the whole earth, to show Himself strong on behalf of those whose heart is loyal to Him."* The Lord loves us all, deeply. But He actively searches for the one who searches for Him. He does not disappoint and the Lord is not a respecter of persons (Acts 10:34 and Romans 2:11).

This holds true for you as much as it does for anyone. It's like the Holy Spirit is a dove circling the sky above actively looking for a place to land. When we keep our hearts fixed on Him and allow Him to claim us entirely, He knows He can trust us with His power. As a result, He uses us, knowing that He alone will get the glory. His dove will land on us and stay!

Sometimes it takes time, as it did for us. But He expects us to take action to prepare. The prophet Habakkuk asked the Lord when He would bring judgment on the wicked. God answered him and said, *"Write the vision and make it plain on tablets, that he may run who reads it. For the vision is yet for an appointed time; but at the end it will speak, and it will not lie. Though it tarries, wait for it; because it will surely come, it will not tarry"* (Habakkuk 2:2). It is not clear from the context what the "vision" was, but it is clear that the Lord answered Habakkuk concerning what was in his own heart in his desire for the purity and holiness of God to be revealed to the nation. The Lord gave him the promise that the vision will eventually be fulfilled and that he should patiently wait for it.

The Lord's timetable is usually longer than ours. Of course, good things can take a while to build. When His time has come and He uses us and begins our ministries, we will be grateful that He did wait. For me, even though He had worked to prepare me, I still felt vulnerable. In those instances, I still feel further preparation may have been more helpful. Nevertheless, He sees things differently. He has His timetable, and we should be grateful for that.

I knew my first trip to Kazakhstan would be an adventure—and I love adventure. I met a young Kazak boy on that trip who, at that time, was 19 years old. He was the younger brother of one of the local pastors. He was tasked to serve as our team's security guard by watching over our team's personal belongings at the house in the village where we were staying. He would stay at the house all day while our team was working. In the evenings, we would fellowship and get to know each other. His name was Daniar. I could tell he loved the Lord and was encouraged by our team, so I befriended him.

The next year, we returned to the village to continue our work and our relationships with the local believers. When we arrived, I learned that Daniar was not able to join us this time. I was disappointed because I had a nice friendship with him and I had looked forward to seeing him again.

I was saddened to learn that a few months back, Daniar had been in a terrible motorcycle accident where he had fractured both his tibia and fibula. These are the two bones in the leg between the knee and ankle. Both were compound fractures, meaning the bones were broken so badly that they penetrated his skin and were visible from the outside.

Immediately after the accident, the fractures were surgically repaired at a local hospital. Shortly after his surgery, the doctors told him that he needed to put weight on his leg and to begin to walk on it again. But when he did, he fell and he fractured the same bones again, and once again the fractured bones ripped through the skin. This required a second surgery, but this time, the surgery was done without anesthesia! Daniar's brother held his hand through the surgery so he could squeeze his brother's hand through the pain.

After the surgery, the doctors installed an external fixator to his leg. This is a medical device commonly used to support a broken bone by immobilizing the joint. It is a metal support structure attached to the outside of his leg, spanning across the joint (in Daniar's case, it spanned across his knee) that would help to hold his bones in place. To install it properly, the surgeons had to drill several holes into his leg bones, above his knee and below the fracture points in his lower leg, so that the fixator could be attached from the outside. The fixator was then attached to his bones with long screws that would hold the structure in place until the bones could heal.

Unfortunately, the surgeons in the village did not have proper equipment and procedures. They were not able to assure the sterility of the equipment when they drilled into the bones. As a result, Daniar's leg became severely infected.

I learned that Daniar could not come to work with us following the accident and the surgeries because he had become very sick due to the bone infection. He had lost about forty-percent of his body weight and he was getting sicker everyday. He had also just experienced septic shock because of the bone infection. Septic shock is the body's reaction to a severe infection and it causes one's blood pressure to become dangerously low. Needless to say, it's a life-threatening condition.

I asked if I could visit Daniar, and his family agreed. They brought Daniar to see us. When Daniar came to our worksite, I was shocked at what I saw. He was so sick, weak, and discouraged. He could barely walk and his infection had progressed to a dangerous level. It was only a few days until our team was to return to America. Although the mission trip was coming to a close, the *real* mission had just begun!

Back home stateside, Daniar was heavy on my heart. I spoke to a friend of mine in our hometown about Daniar's situation who, through a series of contacts, led me to a bone surgeon who agreed to see Daniar for possible surgery. A local hospital agreed to care for Daniar without charge.

My compassion for Daniar was strong, and the doctor's and hospital's willingness to give him medical care for free seemed to me to indicate that the Lord had opened a door to help him. I began working on the administrative details and communications to facilitate his trip to the USA for treatment. As I began this process, it seemed many obstacles arose to challenge this. These circumstantial challenges almost always happen when we move forward with ministry and projects that God has laid on our hearts. Each time a new challenge would arise, it was disheartening to me because it seemed that the situation was bleak and that we would not be able to bring Daniar to the USA for medical care. I wondered, "Why would the Lord allow us to go down the road this far in preparing the way only to see it not work out?" It seemed our vision would fail and our friend whom we loved could die.

One such obstacle was obtaining a visa for a young man who lived in a Muslim village of the country of Kazakhstan, just months after the 911 attacks on US soil. I wondered, *Will Americans, and the American Government, be willing to have him come?* I continued to pray and continued to work, and as I did, we saw the Lord work through these obstacles and challenges one by one.

As each arose, I would pray and declare from His Word that, just as the Lord parted the Red Sea for Moses as he was leading the children of Israel out of Egypt, the Lord would once again part the "sea" in these situations so we could walk through to care for our friend. This is a powerful prayer. I recommend it. The Lord has not forgotten what He did for Israel as they were moving toward His deliverance and promises, and as we declare His Word, it builds faith in our hearts, too. God answers. He did for us, each time.

God does have a plan. But, we will meet resistance to the plan and we have to press forward in order to watch Him fulfill it. This takes work. It takes perseverance to continue in the face of obstacles and it takes faith in declaring His Word in each situation. I encourage you that when you experience what may seem like insurmountable obstacles in moving forward with something God has laid on your heart, pray His Word and declare His Word. I have continued to do this throughout our ministry and continue to see Him move.

In fact, before we continue Daniar's story, I would encourage you to write out a declaration from His Word that would speak faith into the situations you may encounter, and to declare His Word–because His Word is truth. Declare it out loud several times each day until you see a breakthrough. Here is an example that I wrote:

> "Lord, I thank You that Your Word is true (John 17:17). I thank You that You watch over Your Word to perform it (Jeremiah 1:12). I come to You now and I believe in faith that You have a good plan and that You are working now to complete Your plan. The waters of resistance have arisen against us, but we trust Your Word and we know that Your Word is greater than the voice of many waters, and we declare that Your Word is the final word (Psalm 93:3-4). Your Word says, and I declare now, that, "No weapon formed against you shall prosper, and every tongue which rises against you in judgment You shall condemn. This is the heritage of the servants of the Lord, And their righteousness is from Me" (Isaiah 54:17). I declare that as You parted the water of the Red Sea for Moses and the children of Israel to cross safely to the

other side, You can and will part the waters of this situation and allow Your plan to come to completion. You are mighty, God, and You work on behalf of Your children, so I declare in faith that Your Word is true and that You will grant our request for Your Glory. Amen."

When Daniar arrived in the USA, he lived in our home in Raleigh for four months. For most of this time, he was bedridden. The American surgeon surgically removed the infection and the dead tissue from his leg bones, but the battle was not over. His bone infection was still bad and dangerous. An expert physician/infectious disease specialist from the hospital, who also had volunteered his services to help Daniar, told me grimly, "Not only am I uncertain if we can save Daniar's leg, but we are not sure if we can even save his life."

Hearing this was discouraging and concerning. I even wondered, *What will happen if he doesn't make it and he dies here in the USA?* But, throughout this process, we had seen God move and we had a strong sense that Daniar would be okay. We proceeded to follow the course of treatment, which involved giving IV antibiotic treatments. His IV bags were delivered to our home every few days and we were required to change the bags four times each day. After four months, his body was healed of the infection and he was safe to return home, with full use of his leg.

The Lord spared his life and gave us invigorated faith that He would lead us even further in reaching out to help others. We had seen God move and we now know that, despite obstacles that may arise, the Lord would stay with us as we are persistent to stay loyal to Him and the vision He gives us (see II Chronicles 16:9).

The outcome was a victorious one. We believed we had just seen the Lord's true goal for the original mission we had to Kazakhstan. We rejoiced together. But, the mission was not over. What came next was yet more significant. We had seen the Lord give us

His compassion for others as well as an opportunity to help. As we made steps to help, He worked through obstacles and He accomplished His purpose, but we didn't know that this was only the first step.

During the four months that Daniar was with us in our home, we were touched by his living situation in Kazakhstan. His life was placed at risk by improper training and medical equipment. *How many times would this happen to others? If this happened again to Daniar or others, would there be someone there to help them, too?* So, I began to think about how I could help.

I really didn't know how to help. I lacked any experience or specific leading that I could definitively identify as the leading of the Lord. I just had compassion and hoped to help. I simply began to map out what may be necessary to start a medical clinic in his village. After all, the Lord loved the people and we did, too! I had no experience in this and no reason to think that what I had hoped to see is something that I could actually do. But, I loved them, so I started mapping it anyhow. Of course, I asked the Lord if this was Him, and I didn't have an answer yet, but I continued to "write the vision" (see Habakkuk 2:2).

My written plan was not well organized, but it was a beginning. I did not have financial resources, staff, supplies, or the necessary contacts to start it. I simply had hope and a skeleton plan paired with faith that God would do something good for His people.

I shared my thoughts with friends, but just in casual conversation. A few weeks later, I received a phone call from a work colleague who lived in New York. She told me that she had been thinking about what I had shared, and she talked to her dentist friend about it, too. She said that her dentist could procure some dental equipment for us that we could ship it to Kazakhstan for the clinic.

Now, my primary plan had been to start a medical clinic in this village, not a dental clinic. But, when I had written the plan, I included a small dental clinic. It was not the primary function, but simply an ancillary role of the ministry. However, my friend started the process toward the dental side of the vision, so I thought it would be good to continue down that road and see what may develop. I was intrigued, so I also began looking more closely at what we might need to start.

After a short time, I was introduced to a local dentist in my hometown who had also helped to start a dental clinic overseas, and she agreed to help. She connected me to a charity program she knew of that was sponsored by the US State Department. This program no longer exists, but at the time, it was designed to provide direct support to US-based non-profits who were seeking to give medical support supplies to impoverished former Soviet Union nations. *Wow, was that a perfect fit.* Kazakhstan was a former Soviet republic and our goal was to bring medical and dental relief to them.

I applied to the US government agency and was given approval. They agreed to sponsor the costs to send two shipping containers of medical supplies to Kazakhstan! We had to gather the equipment ourselves, but the agency covered the costs of shipment and they handled all of the customs and transportation logistics!

We never did receive any equipment from our friend's dentist in New York—but we didn't need to. Once we shared with others about what we were planning to do, others began donating dental equipment. The donations kept coming. We filled the entire two-car garage in our family's home with modern dental equipment and supplies! We were now *fully* on the hook (if this didn't work, what would I do with all this equipment?). Within just a few months, we packed up and shipped a full-sized forty-foot shipping container of good western dental equipment to Kazakhstan.

As the shipping container was in transit to Kazakhstan, I

began to build a team of volunteers in the USA, including the local dentist, my work colleague, and a representative of the US State Department program, to travel to Kazakhstan to meet the container upon its arrival, to unpack it and set up the clinic. We received permission to renovate the interior of an old warehouse in the village. It became the village dental clinic. I also applied for and received a financial grant from a local company in North Carolina that was willing to help fund the initial operating expenses for the clinic.

Our team arrived in Kazakhstan and we worked for a full week to renovate the warehouse where the clinic would be. We built internal walls and prepared to convert the power supply because the electrical current available in the locale was different from that which was required for our equipment. Unfortunately, the shipping container filled with the equipment experienced some delays in transit and it did not arrive in the village until just a few days before we departed to return home to the United States. So, we scheduled a follow-up trip to finish the work, and we meanwhile planned for the second shipment of supplies from America to Kazakhstan.

Two months later, our second team returned to Kazakhstan and we finished the dental clinic. The grant we had received was sufficient to hire a local Kazakh dentist. An American oral surgeon from our home state, who was a missionary to that region, volunteered his time to help staff the clinic and to train the local dentist whom we had hired. Our dental clinic continued to run for more than 5 years, until this higher standard of dental care became more commonplace for the region, thus decreasing the necessity for the clinic.

When I left for Kazakhstan on the initial mission trip, I had never thought that our compassion for the 19-year-old Kazakh boy would lead to this plan and the eventual clinic. All I knew was that God had given me His heart for the people and that He wanted me to use what I had to take steps toward expressing His love and my love for them. He had already begun the plan, even before I knew it. I simply came to serve, and He did the rest.

We never did start a medical clinic in the village. In many ways, I am glad for this because the complexities of managing the dental clinic project was about all I could manage by myself at that time. The dental clinic was the Lord's plan, but I had to first begin a written plan. Even though the written plan was only partially correct, it nonetheless was a necessary step of faith. As Proverbs 16:3 teaches us, *"Commit to the LORD whatever you do, and He will establish your plans."*

I'm telling you of this journey in starting the clinic for a few reasons. One is to build your faith about what God can do for you. As my pastor used to say, "When you allow Him the space in your heart to move, and you take action to carry it out, He puts His *super* on our *natural* and we see His *supernatural* results." I hope this is encouraging to you, because He will do the same for you, before you even know it.

The second reason I share this with you is that it, too, was only a beginning. It is not the end of the story, but merely a "next step" in His continuing work to build His kingdom and fulfill the vision He put on our hearts. At the time, we didn't know that this was what was happening, but He did. He most certainly will do it for you as you take steps to act today.

He builds His story through you, hope by hope, decision by decision, and action-step by action-step as we endure storms and navigate trails with Him. What God *can* do and what God *will* do has no end.

We must keep a heart to serve and take the next steps in front of us, even if we don't know if those steps may ever be successful. This creates an environment of faith and obedience, and that is what God searches for. Second Chronicles reinforces this by saying, "*The eyes of the LORD run to and fro throughout the whole earth, to show Himself strong on behalf of those whose heart is loyal to Him."* As mentioned earlier, we *must* write the vision that we believe He gives to us, just as He spoke to the prophet Habakkuk: *"Write the vision and make it plain."*

God may bring revisions and tweaks to your plan as you begin to walk in it. You might only have one piece of the puzzle or two. Yet, as you attempt to carry it out, clarity is given. In fact, most of the men and women God raised up in the Bible to do something great only had a fraction of the entire plan when they stepped out. This first step of faith serves as a catalyst for the rest. Doing this not only helps our own hearts and minds to bring clarity to what God is saying, but the act of writing it is a declaration of faith that God will move and establish it. It also helps to make the vision clear to others who may be encouraged to share your vision and help. If it's written, it can be reproduced. If they can understand more clearly what is on your heart, it often encourages them to help. And for them, too, it will begin before they know it.

6

CAPTIVATED BY THE MESSAGE

"For I am not ashamed of the gospel of Christ, for it is the power of God to salvation for everyone who believes, for the Jew first and also for the Greek." (Romans 1:16)

"And without faith it is impossible to please him, for whoever would draw near to God must believe that he exists and that he rewards those who seek him." (Hebrews 11:6)

"For we walk by faith, not by sight." (II Corinthians 5:7)

AS TIME WENT BY, most of my friends and colleagues who had helped to start the clinic either moved away or moved on to new things. I, too, continued my life and career in practicing law. I returned to the daily routine, but my heart was soft to the Lord and I had become what I would term *pregnant* with His vision and compassion for those in need.

My heart looked for the Lord and what He had next. In particular, I began to become aware of how many people throughout the earth not only were unreached by the message of the Gospel, but how many throughout the earth lived in places of isolation. Not only are they unaware of God's salvation plan for them, but they live in places where they actually have no meaningful opportunity to hear the message and respond. Many are trapped in places with governmental borders and spiritual walls such as communism, false religion, and/or economic isolation. In such places, they, as a matter of daily life, are not situated where they will hear the Gospel so that they can respond and receive the Lord.

In western societies, we have places of worship at our disposal every week. However, in many places throughout the world, people have no meaningful opportunity to find a place to hear the Gospel even if they knew such a Gospel may exist. Sadly, among these areas, people regularly pass on to eternity without hearing the name of Jesus or His plan for their salvation and life. In fact, every second of every minute of every hour of every day, someone dies without having even heard the Gospel message.

I became captivated by the message of Romans 10:14, "*How then shall they call on Him in whom they have not believed? And how shall they believe in Him of whom they have not heard? And how shall they hear without a preacher?*" I thought, *Has God called me to be a preacher? Well, maybe.* I didn't seek to be called to preach, but if that is what it takes for others to hear, I thought, *Well, that's okay.*

I pondered this and realized that ministry and the communication of the Gospel message involves a lot more than just a preacher who will proclaim it. In fact, how can a preacher be sent if there is no roadway or bridge for him to travel? I began to think that maybe the Lord will, in fact, use me as a preacher since my heart is for the lost, but even better, maybe He could use my gifts to help facilitate the way and create environments to help make it easier for people to hear the message of the Gospel and to respond to it.

I saw in the Bible how God called Abraham to leave his family roots and travel to a new land, promising to make him a "*great nation,"* and that in him, *"all the families of the earth would be blessed"* (see Genesis 12:1-3). Jesus fulfilled this promise, through His death and resurrection, so that all people may be engrafted into this "great nation," which is the family of God (see Romans 11:17). Before leaving the earth, Jesus commanded us, similar to Abraham, to "go" out from our land and make disciples of all nations (see Mark 16:15). In Revelation, we see the end result, which is a great multitude worshiping God from among *"all nations, tribes, peoples and tongues"* (Revelation 7:9).

I began to see that God has called each of us, individually and together, to fulfill His call to the nations to make disciples, build the body of Christ, and to relieve the burdens of others. This is His call to me, and perhaps it is His call to you, too.

The problem is that the world is lost and separated from God. As a result, so many are left isolated and trapped, unable to hear the message of hope even if they know a message of hope exists. I felt the Lord calling me to be part of the solution. I asked the Lord to please lay on my heart a particular unreached people group of His choosing, somewhere on the earth. In this, I would begin to pray for them to know the Lord, and perhaps I could become part of the solution so that they can hear. As I prayed, I felt the Lord continuing to move in my heart to prepare me for further ministry, but as of yet, I did not have a specific direction as to who this group may be, where they were, or how I could help.

This kind of prayer is a helpful one *if* we have a heart to help, but perhaps a *dangerous* one if we aren't ready to follow through with the answer. God's heart is to establish His Kingdom among every people, tongue, tribe, and nation (Revelation 7:9). His heart is forever fixed on the lost. He is always looking to answer the very prayer that He, Himself, authored in Matthew 9:35-37 and Luke 10:2 when He asked us, His people, to pray for laborers for the harvest. In these verses, the Bible tells us that, *"Jesus went through all the towns and villages, teaching in their synagogues, proclaiming the good news of the kingdom and healing every disease and sickness. When he saw the crowds, he had compassion on them, because they were harassed and helpless, like sheep without a shepherd. Then he said to his disciples, 'The harvest is plentiful but the workers are few. Ask the Lord of the harvest, therefore, to send out workers into his harvest field.'"*

Why is this prayer dangerous if we are not prepared to follow through with the answer? When we pray this, we are coming into agreement with heaven and giving the Lord our word that we are willing to be the answer to this prayer. How could He do anything else but say *yes?* (See Matthew 9:35-37.) This prayer is often dangerous to our current plans. When we do this, He will begin to change the course of our own lives to answer this prayer. We will begin down a new pathway in our lives of having our hearts softened to love the lost, not out of obligation or obedience, but out of His true compassion and love. This begins an alternation of our plans for our own lives. His work will have begun, whether we know it or not.

My wife and I soon felt the Lord nudge us to start a new non-profit organization to serve as the basis for His mission in our lives. We wanted to be prepared for when we had greater understanding into specifically what He wanted us to carry out. I once again began to map out a written plan for that which was on our hearts.

The new organization would carry a name that would reflect what our vision and mission would be. For security reasons, I cannot directly identify our organization's name here, but we will call it *The Pathway to Hearts.* We hoped that *The Pathway to Hearts* would be used as a tool to help build the Kingdom of God among the nations, including unreached people groups that had no reasonable opportunity to otherwise hear the Gospel.

Since I was not a preacher, I contemplated that this new work would be done primarily through the "ministry of mercy"–i.e., demonstrating God's love by extending mercy and help in tangible ways by helping with unmet physical and social needs. We hoped that the Lord would use this to help *plow the ground* to prepare the way for others to come, perhaps with a more defined calling to *preach* the Gospel. This would fulfill the plea of Romans 10:13.

We hoped that as we would *plow* together with mission workers in unreached countries overseas, the Lord would use us to bring Muslims, Buddhists, and other unbelievers into the Kingdom of God and to begin planting permanent works among unreached people groups. We hoped to become a bridge for others to walk who could preach the message of salvation.

THE MEDICAL MANDATE

We began to think that perhaps the primary operating method of this new mercy work in the nations should be that of medical missions. We are not doctors nor medical professionals, but this seemed to make the most sense. I developed and tested a theory to see if I was correct in assuming that this type of ministry would accomplish our purpose. I researched the unreached people groups of the world and the corresponding health conditions in those areas where the unreached live. Interestingly, I learned that if one were to overlay a map of the geographical areas where unreached people groups of the world lived with another map showing the world's greatest health care needs, such as a high infant mortality rate, low median age of death, and availability of reasonably good health care services, the two maps closely match!

This study told me two things: the introduction of the Gospel to an otherwise unreached area brings healing to the people of the land *and* that medical mercy helps to open the door in that area to hearing of the message of the Gospel. I wished to be part of the solution.

I also studied the Bible to see if there may be a direct relationship between a medical mercy mission and the preaching of the message of salvation and healing. I saw that in Matthew 4:23, *"Jesus went about all Galilee, teaching in their synagogues, and preaching the gospel of the kingdom, and healing all manner of sickness and all manner of disease among the people."* Jesus Himself was a medical missionary! Those who saw or experienced this personal touch were challenged by His message to come and follow Him!

I also saw that in Exodus 1:15-21, the Hebrew midwives sheltered the babies of the land from the order of Egypt's Pharaoh to kill them. God used these midwives to save the life of Moses, among others, and Moses was used mightily by God. I like to think that these midwives of Egypt were the first medical team of the Lord! I like to honor them with that thought and I look forward to meeting them in heaven someday and honoring their heroic work!

As a lawyer, I knew that the first step toward developing a new ministry structure would be to form the "Corporate" legal basis for the work. That would require drafting the legal papers and filing them with the government to create a non-profit organization approved by state law, as well as filing a separate application to become qualified as a tax-exempt entity under Section 501(c)3 of the Internal Revenue Code. I began to lay the groundwork for this legal and federal tax-exempt status.

I stepped out in faith to begin the paperwork process as it seemed right in my heart, but I did not want to outpace the Lord as to what steps He had next. As a result, we held off on filing the documents until we had confirmation from the Lord. After all, I was not experienced in ministry and I was not an experienced non-profit organization manager. I only had His heart and a little bit of experience in missions. So, I simply continued to ask Him to confirm these steps; I also continued to pray the "dangerous" prayer that He may perhaps entrust us with a portion of His burden for an unreached group somewhere among the nations.

I always loved medicine, that is, the *field* of medicine. Even when I was a child, maybe like you, I had prepared a "doctor kit" so I would be ready to give medical aid if I may someday come across a person or perhaps an injured animal who might need my care. I used one of my father's old briefcases and I filled it with bandages and other first aid supplies from our home bathroom medicine cabinet. I also made my own chemical laboratory by putting food coloring in different glass jars to play "laboratory." I wanted to be a doctor or a scientist. And, of course, as I described earlier, I sensed someone was always watching—it was the Lord.

While I was in college, I worked as an emergency room technician at a local hospital and as an emergency medical technician for the local ambulance service. I always had an intrigue for the medical field. However, I didn't realize that the Lord was preparing me for this type of work in the mission field. Although I later chose a different career path for my life by becoming a lawyer, the Lord still brought me back to the original passion He placed in my heart when I was a child, for His purposes and for His pleasure. He would use that to answer the "dangerous" prayer I had been praying that I may share His burden for an unreached group in the nations.

Karen and I were very interested in seeing God's hand move in our family and in our world. A popular evangelist visited one of the local churches in our area and we were excited to come to join the event where we were certain to see him move with healings and miracles. During the service, I felt a deep stirring in my heart that the Lord wanted me to lay everything down in my life, even my conceived ideas of ministry and how He would use us. I answered the invitation by the evangelist and I walked to the altar, and with tears, I poured my heart out and laid it down for the Lord. I already knew the Lord, but I felt He was calling me to a deeper level and was bringing a shift in my personal plans. At the altar, I heard the Lord start to speak to me. He started to name countries. I didn't quite know why. I thought that was interesting. I had not thought about these countries before, so I thought that was likely the Lord, and I would keep this in mind to see how He might work.

At the end of the service, I went up front again. This time, I came up to specifically request prayer. I told the pastor that we were at a crossroads in ministry. I told him that we had been involved in a volunteer ministry, but felt He may be leading us to the next step. Yet, I didn't tell him that I had already prepared the legal documents to file with the government to launch *The Pathway to Hearts* as soon as the Lord gave me His "okay." I was hoping that the Lord would confirm this.

Before I finished simply asking for prayer, the pastor stopped me and proceeded to tell me what he began to see in the spirit. He said, "I see a clock on your chest. The hands of the clock are on twelve. The Lord says, 'Now is the time.'" *Wow, I just received the Lord's answer to file the documents!*

But, He wasn't finished yet. The pastor then pointed to my chest and made an arc motion from the right to left, saying, "And I see a pathway. It goes from here" (motioning to the ride side) "...to the hearts" (then motioning to the left side). Not only did we receive confirmation from the Lord that the time to begin was now, but He even directly confirmed the name we had chosen for the organization, *The Pathway to Hearts.*

The pastor told us further that he could see multiple ethnic groups, not just one, and that the Lord would use this ministry as a cutting edge. He said we would see the Lord do things very quickly.

Karen and I both felt the power of the Holy Spirit so strongly that we had trouble continuing to stand up. I felt sure that I would fall down backward as he spoke. It was a powerful moment!

The next day, I filed the Articles of Incorporation (the written documents I had prepared) to begin *The Pathway to Hearts*. This created the corporate legal existence as a nonprofit organization. In a few weeks, I received the formal notice from the Secretary of

State's office that *The Pathway to Hearts* was now established. I then sent the IRS our application for 501(c)3 status, which, if approved, would give us the right to accept donations that the donors could write-off their taxes as tax-exempt donations. It was a very lengthy application that had taken many days to prepare—but we were ready. I filed them and then we needed to wait for our approval for tax exemption from the IRS. This process usually takes between six and eighteen months.

The word the Lord gave us that evening at the church was that we would see Him move very *quickly*. This indeed happened. In less than thirty days, we received a formal written determination from the IRS that our application for tax exemption was *approved*. In less than thirty days, *The Pathway to Hearts* became a legal non-profit organization and was tax exempt. *Amazing!* This was indeed quick. I wondered, *Am I really ready to launch?* This was happening much faster than I thought, but it was as the Lord had said. So, what was next?

Since our legal structure was moving into place quickly, I took the next step to prepare several applications to the State government for the right to use "assumed names" so we could operate our separate programs under distinct names while still under our same corporate banner. We chose assumed names which would support our vision of providing resources to poor local communities and to also provide disaster relief. I needed to have my signature on these applications notarized, so I drove to our neighborhood bank where they had a notary public.

As I drove to the bank, I reached out my hand and placed it on the documents, and I asked the Lord to bless the work these documents will represent and to help us to understand His plan. As I prayed, strangely, the car began to fill with the most beautiful floral fragrance. That had never happened to me before, or since. It was as though my car was quickly and powerfully filled with fresh cut roses. The fragrance was thick and beautiful. That was amazing! When I parked the car at the bank, I lingered inside to continue the experience and wondered what He would do next.

What was that experience? Why did my car fill up with that beautiful fragrance of roses? I am not totally sure. But I do know that in the book of Ruth, the Bible refers to Solomon's wife as the Rose of Sharon. Sharon is a rather large plain in Palestine that is known for its beautiful flowers. The book of Ruth is a romantic story that many believe is an allegory of the relationship between Christ and the Bride of Christ, namely, His church. Did He just fill my car with His scent? The Rose of Sharon? Was He again confirming His plan?

The next week, I returned to my job. All was as usual, except I awaited the Lord's next step. I knew He had spoken to me listing different countries, most of which I had never before considered. The chief among them was China. Why would God use me in China? After all, years ago, during my Sunday school class as a young lawyer, as mentioned earlier, I asked my wife, "Why would anyone want to go to China? That's the last place I would want to go."

One morning at work, I was walking down the hall and passed by the entry door into our law department's breakroom. The breakroom was small and it consisted of a few vending machines, a water supply tank, a coffee pot, a refrigerator, and a few cabinets. On the wall, there was a map of the world and a small table in front of it. Our law department was quite a social group and we enjoyed sharing our lives with each other. Our department staff had the practice of placing thumb tacks with our individual names taped onto them, onto the map in the breakroom, identifying the states and/or countries where we had planned to visit on our vacations that year. It was fun to see where everyone planned to go so we could enjoy that together. It was now springtime, so the thumbtacks were beginning to appear now that everyone's vacation plans were starting to firm up.

As I walked past the breakroom, I glanced in, just as I had casually done many times before. This time it was different. My eyes instantly went to the map on the wall, because for some very strange reason, I saw the words *OPEN DOOR* appear as though they were literally burned into the map. The words appeared directly over the country of China!

What did I just see? What does this mean? I looked again. This time, the map looked as normal as it always did. I saw the country of China, but I didn't see the burned-in words *OPEN DOOR*. I thought, *Did I really just see that?* I certainly thought I did, and especially since China was not on my mind at that moment; I was merely passing by the room.

I walked back past the breakroom several more times that day just out of curiosity as to whether I would see that again, or something similar; or maybe to learn that it may have been some strange reflection. It wasn't. The words did not appear again, but I knew what I saw. That evening, I told Karen about that experience.

The next Sunday morning, our family went to church as usual. Our church was a forty-five minute drive from our home. It was a bit far, but we had joined the church before our first home in Raleigh had burned down, and when we moved, we didn't want to leave it. So, we would usually have to leave for church quite early just to make sure we arrived on time, in the event that we hit traffic. Sometimes it was difficult to leave early since we had four children and not everyone could get ready on time.

This Sunday, we were not late. We arrived about ten minutes before the service started. When we entered the front door and stood in the foyer, I saw an old friend whom I had not seen for several years. She and her family used to attend the church, but they had left the church a few years prior, so it was a delight to see her. I walked up to greet her. She immediately told me that the reason she was there that morning was because she wished to speak to me and that it was urgent. What she asked me next left me with my mouth wide open in surprise. She said to me, "You brought teams of people to Kazakhstan to build the dental clinic. Can you please bring a team to China?"

China? I thought. *Did she really just ask me this?* I had previously asked the Lord to put an unreached people group on my heart. I had later heard Him whisper a list of countries in my ear, the chief one being China. I had received the prophetic word from the Lord that He would send us to a place of multiple ethnic groups and that things would happen quickly. Earlier that week, I had passed the breakroom and saw *OPEN DOOR* burned into the map over the country of China! And now I am being asked to come to China?

I replied to her decisively, "Yes, I will." But I said that first I needed to go there to see what the project is before I can bring a team. She said, "Great, we leave in three weeks. I'll alert the group in China and get you set up as part of the team." I thought, *Wow, did that really happen? He said it would happen fast.* It did. Three weeks later, I was traveling to China to see what the Lord had for us there.

When I left for China, I knew the basic itinerary, but I didn't know the trip details nor did I know much about the nation itself. Specifically, I didn't know that China was a melting pot in Eastern Asia of multiple ethnic groups, including 56 designated minority groups that are formally recognized by China. This means that these 56 groups originated as a distinct culture, either from outside of China or from within China as the nation grew as a country. I also did not know that as China grew and the Gospel message became known within China, it still had not penetrated into the cultures and hearts of all of these 56 groups. Some of them were, and still are, listed as *unreached people groups* with fewer than 97% who know the Lord or have heard the Gospel message. I also didn't know that our trip to China was a rare outreach to the most unreached ethnic group in the province of China.

You may not know yet what God has intended for your life, but I believe that you have the sense that He does have a plan and wishes to use you. I would encourage you to pray this "dangerous" prayer if you are ready for Him to answer it:

> "Lord Jesus, thank You that You love the unreached of this world. Thank You that You paid the price for their redemption and that You desire to use Your people as part of Your plan to reach them. Lord, I place my life in Your hands. Please use me for Your plan. Lord, I invite You to captivate my heart with Your Gospel message of salvation for the lost. I invite You to place on my heart a group or groups that are unreached and who don't know Your name, and I invite You to show me what I can do to help reach them. Please send laborers into Your harvest field to bring souls into Your kingdom, and please prepare me and send me, too."

As we pray what is already on His heart, the Lord will begin to develop our understanding of His plan for us personally to be the answer to what you have prayed for. When He does this, it is important to begin to write down the plan and vision that you see in your heart. Again, this will likely change over time, but you will need to begin somewhere. Now would be a good time to begin. You can revise it from time to time, and it will become a declaration of faith on your part that God is at work to fulfill His purposes in you.

7

BE CAREFUL ABOUT WHAT YOU AGREE TO

"For all the promises of God in Him are Yes, and in Him Amen, to the glory of God through us." (II Corinthians 1:20)

"Without faith it is impossible to please God." (Hebrews 11:6)

THE PROVINCE where we work is an arid region close to the southwestern border of the Gobi Desert. It is located close to the geographical center of China, but it is typically referenced as being in northwest China due to the location of China's historical boundaries and its culture. It is considered a drought region due to low annual rainfall.

The Silk Road passes through this region. Historically, travelers and merchants from other countries would enter China by way of the Silk Road and proceed along the road as a trading route. The Great Wall of China also extends to the northern part of the province, but much of it has deteriorated in this region so it is not one of the more popular tourist locations for the Great Wall. In fact, there is very little tourism in the province at all.

Instead, it is a territory of a humble life for its citizens, some who live in cities and many more who live in the rural and mountainous villages. The province is home to a considerable number of diverse Chinese minority groups, including the Hui, Mongols, Tibetans, and Kazaks. Most importantly, it is home to the minority groups that the Lord led us to in order to show them His love. I will leave them unnamed for now so as not to hinder the work among them, which continues yet still.

The history of these people is not certain. It is believed that, in the thirteenth century when China was subdued by the Mongols, Genghis Khan moved some of his garrison units into China. These soldiers then intermarried and developed into their own distinct ethnic group and continue to reside in the area. Another theory is that when Kublai Khan invaded central Asia in the mid-1200s AD, the population of the invaded area migrated into this area to avoid war. Either way, the people of this group have retained their distinct identity as an ethnic minority in China, and they are highly unreached.

The villagers here are poor. They are primarily farmers, and their main crops are potatoes, barley, wheat, and corn. Many of them live in mud-structured houses. There are yet others we have visited who actually still live in cave-houses which were manually dug into the side of a mountain.

Although China sadly prides itself of having no official religion (except atheism), the minority groups are generally allowed to practice their own religion so long as doing so does not interfere with the Government's management of the people. The ethnic group we work with are mostly Muslim. As such, the mountainous region is filled with small- and medium-sized mosques, most of which have an architectural similarity to the mosques of the Middle East. This is because much of the funding for theses ornate mosques which are scattered throughout this poor region came from the richer Muslim nations in the Middle East.

As the people have continued their ethnic traditions and

culture without integrating into mainstream Chinese society, their isolation has led to a mistrust of the ethnic Chinese majority – typically referred to as the Han. This mistrust is ever deeper toward foreigners. There are several reasons for this, but those are not important to explore for the purposes of this book. The important thing to know is that in order to gain acceptance and credibility to speak the message of the Gospel to the people, the Gospel must first be demonstrated by love, and one must first gain trust and relationship. The people of this area do not quickly embrace and accept anything from outsiders. Many have tried this before, some with limited degrees of success. Currently, there are very few Christian believers in this region, and the nearest church they could visit is in the closest city more than an hour away by car.

When I visited China for the exploratory trip, our team first met in Hong Kong to join up with about forty others who had traveled from many different nations for the purpose of reaching out to the Chinese. This was in 2004. After a few days of preparation, we divided into separate teams to travel to various areas of China for different purposes. The team I joined was sent to serve this unreached group and the orphan children in a proximate region. That is where and when I met the leader of this operation, who eventually would become a mentor and a spiritual dad to me. His love for the Chinese is profound and his experience in China is deep. He traveled with me and our group to northwest China and introduced me to the leader of a local organization he had founded.

While serving on the team, I found myself once again tasked with the humble role of physical labor. This time, instead of digging a latrine, I helped pull weeds in a local farmer's potato field. I felt the Lord encouraging me that He would use me spiritually at some point, just as He was using me in this physical labor. I was able to meet with the chief representative of the local NGO (non-governmental organization) and share my vision for medical outreach to the unreached among the nations. Although she was a bit skeptical, she invited me to bring a medical team to China the following year. I returned to the United States to prepare for the next steps.

I was not connected with the medical community, but I knew the Lord wanted me to gather a medical team to reach out, on-site, to the people in this remote area of China. I didn't know if doctors would be willing to join or if others would be willing to help. But, I felt that it was the Lord's prompting, so I proceeded to do as I thought He had said.

The Lord gave me a passage from Isaiah 62:10 which helped to clarify the focus of our call to help in the region:

> "Go through,
> Go through the gates!
> Prepare the way for the people;
> Build up,
> Build up the highway!
> Take out the stones,
> Lift up a banner for the peoples!"

I felt the Lord wanted to use us to work in various nations, including China, by preparing the means for others to come and serve. We were to build up a metaphorical highway by laying the foundation for others overseas to travel to the unreached areas. He wanted us to help remove the barriers to ease the way for others to come who otherwise wouldn't be able to. Perhaps even some would come to preach the good news of the Gospel.

In order for us to build up a highway and remove the stones, so to speak, we had to know some basic information, like where the road was supposed to be and how to get there. We had to know what the barriers were and how to remove them. For us and for this project, there was a lot of work and experience ahead of us that we needed to gain in order to do this successfully. But how does someone get to that point and gain the personal preparations needed before starting?

We generally don't know the answers to all of our questions before we begin. Sometimes ministry development is less a matter of following a plan item-by-item than it is holding onto the Lord for dear life. Sometimes He leads us to make decisions and follow paths when we don't know where it is going or what the outcome may look like. It's like following a map that is folded in the center so you can only see part of the journey, but not the end. This is the way He intends for things to work, because if we knew the destination or the result, it would not take faith on our part to get there. This is vital because, "*Without faith it is impossible to please God*" (Hebrews 11:6).

And further, sometimes we are not sure that a particular idea or path that we think we should take is precisely what His next step really is. In those cases, if we set out too early, we risk a costly mistake, but if we proceed too late, we may miss the opportunity. What do we do then? Do we do nothing and just wait? Or do we move forward in faith and take the risk? This is something that we all must wrestle with. There is no hard and fast answer to those questions. Yet, in the end, it is important to understand that the Lord knows where we are and knows what we can see and what we cannot see.

The Lord knows what He is asking us to do and what we, personally, need from Him in order to confirm this to us. He does want us to take steps of faith, but He also wants us to use the good sense He has given to us to make wise decisions. As we step out in faith, with a righteous intent, the Lord gives us a great safety net of grace. He also holds us into account to exercise the wisdom that we already have. How this plays out is a balance. This is yet another reason we must seek Him and allow Him to steer us.

INITIAL PREPARATIONS

I prepared a brief written pamphlet describing a medical outreach team that I hoped to bring to this minority ethnic group in China. My wife and I gave the pamphlet to a few trusted friends for them to perhaps share with other people they may know who might be interested in joining. I didn't know who might see the brochure. One of the people we gave the pamphlet to was a nurse-friend of my wife who worked at the fitness center of a local hospital system.

A few days later, I was in my car driving home from work and I received a call on my cell phone from a doctor in Raleigh. He told me that, earlier that day, he was exercising on the treadmill at the hospital fitness center, while meditating on Romans 8:28, and that a nice nurse came and asked him, "Dr. Art, would you like to go to China?" Dr. Art told her, "Sure, I'll go." She then gave him the brochure.

I met with Dr. Art for dinner later in the week. He brought his wife, who, as it turned out, was also a doctor. I shared my vision with them and learned that they had similar work in the Philippines. They agreed to join me in China for our medical mission.

During our dinner, I shared with him that I'd also like to offer surgery as a part of our medical team. So, they invited me to dinner the next week and brought their surgeon-friend, who also participates in their Philippines mission. The surgeon agreed to come to China, too. To my amazement, the surgeon said, "I'll bring my nephew who is a surgeon, my niece who is a nephrologist, and my other niece who is an emergency physician." *How many doctor-family members does this man have?* As it turned out, he had far more yet.

So, our next steps were clear: to prepare and bring the medical team to serve the unreached minority group in northwest China. God even provided the medical staffing to start. I looked back at how the Lord put this together and all He had taken us through to get this far. It was like solving a mystery by reading a book backwards, seeing the outcome, and then reviewing and seeing how it all came together. That is, because His work had begun before I knew it.

The first medical team went very well. We were encouraged, so we planned for a second one for later that summer. In fact, we continued this trend and held two medical teams each year for the next fifteen years. Not all of the teams were located in this particular region, but all of them served the unreached communities in the poor villages of the province.

Our medical teams now average about 120 people from twelve different countries, all who serve the same heart purpose–to express the love of God to demonstrate His heart for the people. The result is that we see Muslims, Buddhists, Atheists, and others come to the Lord. Sometimes members of our own medical teams come to the Lord. But importantly, the teams also include local Chinese believers who are able to serve these unreached people in a more direct and ongoing way than we would ever be able to do.

When our medical teams began, we consisted almost entirely of foreigners, and the Chinese people looked upon us with interest and humor. Over time, the Chinese people began to become more involved. Now, each of our teams consist of more Chinese people than people from all other countries combined. It is a beautiful thing to see. It is almost like a part of heaven from Revelation 7:9-10, "*After this I looked, and behold, a great multitude that no one could number, from every nation, from all tribes and peoples and languages, standing before the throne and before the Lamb, clothed in white robes, with palm branches in their hands, and crying out with a loud voice, 'Salvation belongs to our God who sits on the throne, and to the Lamb!'*"

I continued to organize and manage the China medical teams while I was still living in the United States and practicing law. After a few years, the NGO's chief representative resigned from the ministry for personal reasons, and the NGO's Board asked me, personally, if I would consider moving to China to take her lead role. I agreed. In 2012, I resigned my position as legal counsel for the pharmaceutical company, and my wife and I moved to China to serve full-time. Neither of us spoke Chinese, and neither of us were trained in missions. Neither of us had EVER thought we would move to China. After all, "That was the last place [we] would ever want to go."

Before I left my job and moved to China, I would have my morning devotions in my home office before I left for the 45-minute drive to work for the day. I would usually recline in my office chair with my feet on my desk and a nice cup of hot coffee in my hand. I would take the time to pray and read His Word before beginning the day.

If we are to begin in ministry, this is a habit we all must master. It is not always easy, especially when you work full-time, have a family full-time, and you try to serve as you can and hold some semblance of a balanced life! But as a wise man once told me, "Everything worth doing is worth doing right." Culturing a relationship with the Lord is worth doing! It is a necessary relationship if we are to endure the spiritual and practical challenges along the way.

One morning with my feet on my desk and coffee in hand, I first scanned the headline news on my computer. I was particularly struck by an urgent news flash. A young Korean-American man was reported to have crossed the border from China into North Korea to give a personal message to Kim Jong-il, the then-current dictator of North Korea. His message for the dictator was to stop his violation of human rights. He never got to deliver the message because he was arrested and imprisoned, and we later learned he was tortured.

That was all the news that was announced at that point, as it was a developing story. I had heard of the brutality of the North

Korean regime. I knew that North Korea was not a safe place and was not open to foreigners, and that Christians were imprisoned or martyred for their faith.

So, with coffee in hand, I prayed for the young man. I prayed, **"Lord, thank You that I am not called to North Korea."** Yup, those were the first words out of my mouth. Not only was I struck with how selfish that was of me, but the words of my prayer echoed what I had said years earlier: **"Why would anyone want to go to China? That's the last place I'd want to go."** The remembrance of those earlier words about China filled my head and my heart. Did I just challenge the Lord again? I repented and said, "Lord, I'm sorry. If You ever wish to call me to North Korea, I will go."

Again, I learned, "It started before I knew it." One of my friends had already invited me to have dinner one evening that week with an acquaintance of his who had an active ministry in China and who would be traveling through our town. So, as a matter of courtesy and honor, we looked forward to meeting him for a time of fellowship and encouragement over the work in China.

That evening came and we did talk about China. In fact, China had become one of my favorite topics to discuss and it was great to be in the company of colleagues who shared my same passion. But the line of conversation turned sharply, when out of the blue he asked me a question I didn't expect: "Would you consider sharing the Lord's burden for North Koreans and come to northeastern China? We will reach out to the North Koreans who have escaped North Korea and who are living in the border region in China."

It felt like déjà vu. Earlier that week, I had challenged the Lord as to where I did and did not want to go, and just as my friend had asked in the foyer of our church a few years prior, "Will you come to China?" this man now asked me, "Will you come to help the North Korean people?"

I felt the presence of the Lord in a strong way. One way that the Lord shows me His presence is that sometimes my heart, for no other apparent reason, will start to beat fast. This happened at that moment. Strangely, my eyes began to fill with tears. I was taken off-guard and then I tried to gather myself to ask the only reasonable or dignified thing I could think of to say. I felt I needed to say at least something. So, I asked, "Um, what are their needs?"

His answer was, "Well, that depends upon whether or not they have been tortured." Well, that did it, we were all in tears at that point. The Lord's heart was strongly present. I told him, "Yes," and he agreed to have his personal friend who had an ongoing work in North Korea to contact me shortly. His friend did contact me, and within just a few months, he and I visited North Korea together for a discrete and special project. Please forgive me, I cannot explain here about the details of those trips.

The point of my telling you about the North Korean initiative is that one step leads to another, and *that* step leads to another. You will not get to the later steps until you take the first ones. And you will not get to the first steps until your heart is prepared to obey the Lord and is willing to take the personal risks and make the personal sacrifices that are necessary to get there. You might just need to say, "Yes," and agree to the next step, even if it is not one that you intended to take.

The journey is a long one and it is not easy. The journey may have different legs, and each of those may be discrete with varying lengths and purposes. Yet, they each tie-in to each other and each is not the end of the story. Each is only the beginning because the story will continue to be written for so long as you are willing to obey and carry His burden. The story of ministry development is a progressive story, and no one sees the result or the end before they start. In fact, you usually don't even see these things *as* you walk through it. It is a walk of faith that we must all agree with the Lord to take day-by-day, week-by-week, month-by-month, and year-by-year, without knowing the full picture or the end.

Sometimes the next steps He wants us to take are obvious, and sometimes they are not. Sometimes they are easy and sometimes they are difficult. At times, we have to take them reluctantly. The Lord tells us that His yoke is easy and His burden is light (see Matthew 11:30). I can tell you that His burden is also deep, and His burden is enduring, and He seeks those who are willing to share it with Him. He will only share it with those He trusts to endure to see it to the end.

Are you willing? Are you willing to carry His heart to a people and place, and in circumstances that you had never envisioned? Are you willing to share His burden? If so, will you allow Him to test you and try your heart? Are you willing to agree with His next step, even if it is one that was not in your plan?

Would you please join me now and pray this prayer that King David prayed to the Lord in Psalm 139? Please read and pray this out loud to let it soak into your heart, and please journal in your personal notes that you have prayed this today! This will be important as you see the Lord's answer to the prayer unfold in your life. Am I convinced of this? Yes. Please pray this out loud:

> "O Lord, You have searched me and known me.
> You know my sitting down and my rising up;
> You understand my thought afar off.
> You comprehend my path and my lying down,
> And are acquainted with all my ways.
> For there is not a word on my tongue,
> But behold, O Lord, You know it altogether.
> You have hedged me behind and before,
> And laid Your hand upon me.
> Such knowledge is too wonderful for me;
> It is high, I cannot attain it.

Where can I go from Your Spirit?
Or where can I flee from Your presence?
If I ascend into heaven, You are there;
If I make my bed in hell, behold, You are there.
If I take the wings of the morning,
And dwell in the uttermost parts of the sea,
Even there Your hand shall lead me,
And Your right hand shall hold me.
If I say, 'Surely the darkness shall fall on me,'
Even the night shall be light about me;
Indeed, the darkness shall not hide from You,
But the night shines as the day;
The darkness and the light are both alike to You.
For You formed my inward parts;
You covered me in my mother's womb.
I will praise You, for I am fearfully and wonderfully made;
Marvelous are Your works,
And that my soul knows very well.
My frame was not hidden from You,
When I was made in secret,
And skillfully wrought in the lowest parts of the earth.
Your eyes saw my substance, being yet unformed.
And in Your book they all were written,
The days fashioned for me,
When as yet there were none of them.
How precious also are Your thoughts to me, O God!
How great is the sum of them!
If I should count them, they would be more in number
than the sand;
When I awake, I am still with You.
Oh, that You would slay the wicked, O God!
Depart from me, therefore, you bloodthirsty men.
For they speak against You wickedly;

our enemies take Your name in vain.
Do I not hate them, O Lord, who hate You?
And do I not loathe those who rise up against You?
I hate them with perfect hatred;
I count them my enemies.
Search me, O God, and know my heart;
Try me, and know my anxieties;
And see if there is any wicked way in me,
And lead me in the way everlasting.
Amen!"

If you prayed this with me, I am convinced that the Lord will continue His work in revealing His destiny for your life and will use all that you have submitted to His feet. Sometimes we don't realize what we actually have and what we can actually do until He asks us to do it. Remember, His work has *already begun.*

8

LET DOWN YOUR NETS...ALL OF THEM

> "When He had stopped speaking, He said to Simon, 'Launch out into the deep and let down your nets for a catch.' But Simon answered and said to Him, 'Master, we have toiled all night and caught nothing; nevertheless, at Your word I will let down the net.'" (Luke 5:4-5)

> "I planted, Apollos watered, but God gave the increase..." (I Corinthians 3:6)

SOME OF THE things the Lord has asked us to do are things in which we had no formal training. Yet, as we obeyed, even though we were not trained for it, we look back and see that He instead had uniquely equipped us for the task in ways we had not considered.

Sometimes He calls us to things that He equips us for along the way. A friend of mine used to tell me that, "God doesn't call those who are equipped but He equips those whom He calls." Although He does use experiences we have throughout life in ways that we did not expect, He does require us to rely on Him.

Not only that, but He causes us to learn what we need to know, when we need to know it, and enables us with the resources we need for His work. He is always on time. As you may have heard, God is never late; but He does miss opportunities to be early.

His ways are not always logical (in the way that we measure logic), however, they always make sense in the end. As I mentioned in the last chapter, working with the Lord is sometimes like holding on for dear life, as He brings us from one step to the next. The walk of a servant of the Lord is not an easy walk. It is full of joy along the way, but it is also hard work and can be very physically, emotionally, and spiritually draining.

God asked Moses to lead the children of Israel out of Egypt to deliver them and to bring them to a land of promise. That said, why was their first stop in the journey the banks of the Red Sea—where they were pinned against the sea with the violent Egyptian Army closing the distance? Did He lead them into an onslaught? With what they thought would be a blessing, did God actually mean it to be a trap? Of course not. It didn't make logical sense... *but it did.* When God parted the water, it showed them God's redemption and gave them courage for the rest of the journey which would see yet even more difficult situations.

Jesus also asked His disciples to do odd things from time-to-time. One time, Jesus had been teaching a multitude of His followers and used a boat that belonged to one of His disciples to stand on as a platform. After the teaching, He told his disciple, *"Launch out into the deep and let down your nets for a catch"* (Luke 5:4). His disciple thought this made no sense at all because he had been fishing all day and caught nothing. Nonetheless, he obeyed, and as a result, caught so many fish that his nets nearly broke (Luke 5:5-6).

There will be times when He will have you step out in faith like Moses did, and the environment around you will seem unsure. There will be other times when He may nudge you to take a next step at an unseemly time. It could be that He asks you to do something you've already tried, like when He asked Peter to let down his nets for a catch. Or, sometimes, it may be the logical next step to take, or even a step that you have no choice in, so you hold your breath and jump in!

One example of this is when I was serving on the ministry board and agreed to take over the position of Chief Representative for the work in China. This required me to leave my job as a lawyer and take on a new responsibility, overseas, without pay. It was a volunteer position. And I had a family at home. Three of our four children had already grown and were either in college or had finished college and were on their own. Our youngest son was still in high school.

During the board meeting where I accepted this invitation, I had a lot to consider all at once. But in the end, I knew the Lord had called me to this work, and if I did not accept the invitation, the work in China would be closed. So, I took the plunge and agreed. I would leave my career as a lawyer with a great salary and future potential that could have funded many different works overseas, and instead go to China to work in a land where I did not know the language to do things I had never done before.

After I made the decision and communicated the step of faith that we would take, one of our team's intercessors, who was quite prophetic, had a dream. She said she saw me walking across water that was turbulent with weather and waves. There were wood pilings in the water. Pilings are wooden poles, like telephone poles, that are sometimes driven into the ground underwater to help support a structure like a boat dock. In her dream, the pilings were placed in the water in a pattern such that I could step on them one at a time, but it was very hard to see exactly where they were. But as I would take the next step, I would see where the next piling was and so I was able to safely place my foot on it. I was able to step across the water one piling at a time, each step being a step of faith that the next one would appear. This was such a helpful illustration to fall back on when things got difficult in ministry. The Lord has definitely directed us to take steps in situations that we knew were risky, but He has always come through.

One of the factors that I had to consider in making this decision was our ability to meet our family's personal financial needs. I would not have an income from the ministry and I did not have a lot of money in savings to live on—nor did I qualify for retirement yet as the Lord asked me to leave my job five years before I would qualify for the company's retirement plan. Where would the funds come from? This was a step of faith in search for the next piling to step on in the water.

At the time I left my job, I had put aside enough money that our family could live on comfortably for about six months. After that, we would have to see what God would do. I formulated a plan for raising funds through donations into *The Pathway to Hearts* that would be designated for our personal support. I had no idea if I would be successful or if donated funds would be sufficient to even cover any of the ministry's financial needs, let alone ours. If they were not, I would need to return back to secular employment.

When walking through this, I was reminded by my spiritual dad of the words Derek Prince spoke while addressing the scenario of trusting the Lord for resources for ministry. He said, "God's work done God's way will never lack God's resources." Think about that! It may seem simple, but it is profound. Derek Prince was one of the world's leading Bible teachers and his teachings have had a deep impact on us and our ministry work. In fact, our ministry was birthed out of Derek's ministry as it was founded by one of his direct disciples.

These words I was reminded of have held true. We have been working in full-time ministry, without secular employment, for almost ten years and we have never lacked the resources we needed, when we needed them. If we knew in advance where our funding would come from, we may have felt more secure. But, we would not have had to step out in faith trusting God to supply. Had we missed that challenge of waiting and trusting in faith, we would not have had the beautiful experiences of seeing His hand supply our need and the testimony of how He stays faithful to His promises. It also helped build our faith to take yet larger steps. God is faithful and will always provide the next piling for the next step.

Another example is when my wife and I first moved to China to assume the work, and we were almost immediately left without administrative or language support. When we had agreed to move, we relied on the fact that the organization's administrative assistant, who was a wonderful Chinese woman who had worked for the organization since its beginning about twelve years earlier, would be there to help us. She knew all of the ropes about when and how the company was to complete its annual government registration requirements, how our visas would be maintained, and how to keep the company's records. She was the one who knew who to call for transportation from one project to the next. These were all very important tasks and we were grateful to have her there because we could not handle these matters ourselves in a new situation in a new country, and with a language we did not know. She was also to serve as our translator since we had never taken Chinese lessons before, as we never thought we were actually going to move to China.

However, shortly after we arrived in China to make the official move, our administrative assistant informed us that she was pregnant and was leaving her work for six to nine months of maternity leave. She and her husband would be having a second child. At that time, it was very unusual for families in China to have more than one child. But, our work was located in the farming region of northwestern China, where China allowed multiple children so that families could get the help they needed on the family farms. Our assistant was not from a farming family, but nonetheless she was permitted to have a second baby without penalty or forced abortion.

We thought it was wonderful that she would have a second baby, except for the fact that she told us she was now leaving her work with us to go on maternity leave and would be unable to help us in translation or administrative matters for at least six months. She never did return to work because, shortly afterwards, she and her husband moved to a different area. She left her employment with us completely.

We were stunned! We were in a foreign land, with a foreign language, and we did not know how to maintain the company's standing or projects. We were being asked to take yet another step in the turbulent waters in hopes that the next pilling would appear.

We looked for the next piling. It was Sunday, so Karen and I decided to go to a local restaurant for lunch. This too was a step of faith not having help even to order the food. We decided to enjoy the local specialty of noodles. In China, it seems that every region and city is famous for a particular type of food. Food is very important to the Chinese! All throughout China our city is known for its specialty noodle dish, which is quite unique in composition and taste, and many restaurants exist that serve nothing but this noodle dish. I didn't enjoy beef noodles when we first arrived in China, but I have come to enjoy it very much.

The beef noodle shop was busy and there seemed to be no place for us to sit down. I went up to the order window to pick up our noodle bowls while Karen searched for a place for us to sit down to eat. She finally found a table that had two empty seats. So, I brought the noodle bowls to her table so we could begin our lunch.

When we sat down, we heard the most beautiful sound we

could imagine that day. English! The Chinese lady we had sat next to spoke wonderful English. The first words she said to us were, "Are you guys Christians?" I was just as stunned over the question as I was over hearing it in English.

I thought, *Oh no, is it safe to answer that question in a Muslim restaurant in a place where Christianity is not welcomed and it was illegal for foreigners to share their faith?* Well, it is *never* wise to deny knowing the Lord (II Timothy 2:12) so I answered and said, "Yes, we are Christians." She told us that she was a Christian, too. Her English name was Sarah.

Sarah told us that she actually lived in a different place in the city. She had not planned to come to that noodle shop for lunch that day. But, she had been waiting for her bus to arrive at the street corner so that she could get on the correct bus that would go near her home. Instead, a different bus stopped first, but she got on it by mistake. This bus stopped in front of this noodle shop, so she got off and decided to eat there until she could go back and find the correct bus to take her home. The Lord sent her to us! He knew we needed someone with a familiar language and the encouragement of knowing there were believers in the area to connect with.

We were excited to have a new friend, but we didn't know just how significant this introduction would be. During lunch, we talked about our work and how we had arrived in China only to learn that our administrative assistant was leaving. We explained that our administrative support and language support were now gone, and we were left with an immediate and important need for help. We asked her if she would be interested in filling the open position. She told us that she could not take the position, but she promised us that she would try to find someone who could. We appreciated her gesture of support. After lunch, we traded phone numbers with her and we departed to our respective homes.

We continued to pray that the Lord would quickly provide the right person to work for us in China. We were able to get some temporary help for translation a few times, but not a regular employee.

One day, we had traveled to a different region for a project. We were in the driver's car and I received a phone call. Although I did not speak Chinese, I answered the call anyhow. It was Sarah! Sarah said, "I found a worker for you." She said that the person's name was Lily. She did not know Lily personally, but she had spoken to several of her friends about a need for someone to work for us, and each time, she was directed to Lily. She was told that Lily was a Christian and was available to work, and they each recommended her. Sarah then contacted Lily who agreed to meet with us for a job interview.

When Lily came to our apartment to meet us for the interview, we immediately liked her. We offered her the job and she accepted. The Lord provided us a person to serve alongside who loved Him, was eager to grow in Him, and who was very able to handle the job. We were excited.

Lily quickly learned the role and displayed a beautiful heart for the Lord and for ministry. She was instrumental in helping us expand the work due to her keen insights and her trust and confidence in the Lord. She grew in the Lord greatly.

The thought occurred to me one day, "I'll bet my oldest son, Andrew, would really like Lily, and I hope that perhaps she would like him, too." To me, it seemed like they might be a good match for each other. They lived on complete opposite ends of the globe, but both loved the Lord and both had a heart for missions. Our son Andrew had served as a leader at the YWAM base in Kona, Hawaii, and he led teams overseas.

Andrew had begun helping me with a new addition to our ministry work. We had decided to begin a small coffee shop which would serve as an opportunity to further reach the emerging generation of Chinese who were hungry for something greater than themselves, and would also provide a platform for our continued work in China in the event China would no longer approve visas for foreign NGO workers like ourselves. We had heard rumors that the involuntary closure of NGOs had already begun, so we had to pay careful attention to be sure we were laying the groundwork necessary for the continued work in case this happened to us.

Andrew traveled to China to help me, and in doing so, he met Lily. The two of them hit it off quite well. I'll leave the rest of this story for them to tell. But I will tell you that after four years of serving us and the ministry in China, Lily became our daughter-in-law and the mother of our first grandchild. Andrew and Lily have moved to America, so we sadly lost Lily as our full-time worker, but we gained her as part of our family forever!

This was yet another example of how the Lord used obstacles and challenges that we thought would be impossible to surmount instead be for our blessing and to help us move closer to His destiny! He used yet another situation that did not logically seem to fit into the overall plan of ministry that we expected. Nonetheless, we accepted this and stepped forward in faith. Through the obstacles, He was able to show how He overcomes them and had His hand in the situation the whole time. He had already begun the plans to move Lily into our lives, but we had to walk through the obstacles in faith to see it!

ACQUIRING TRAINERS

Before we moved to China, when I was leading our early medical teams in China, I was in the process of searching for and buying portable dental equipment for our teams. This type of field-based dentistry required specialized equipment and technique. Dentistry is very supply-intensive. There are so many varied instruments and supplies that are necessary to have on hand before a dentist can really do much of anything. So, field-based dentistry must be flexibly-equipped in a creative way to adapt to different circumstances, while minimizing the volume of equipment and expense in order to stay mobile. This took a lot of my personal time and research, while I was still working as a lawyer. I wasn't sure what the eternal importance of this was, but nonetheless took it seriously, so I learned and I worked.

As I was in the process of finalizing the purchases, I was on the phone with a supplier of equipment. He asked me, "What is it you are doing in China?" I told him that we have access to a poor and unreached group and were using dentistry as a means to help them with their needs and to reach their hearts. He replied and told me that his company had a heart for China. He went on to say that his company had worked in other countries and had brought training in dentistry to indigenous believers who were interested and apt to learn it.

I found that very interesting given that I had just had a discussion with my counterpart in China who told me that a Chinese group of believers in another area had a heart for the local village people, but they needed an approved, legitimate trade in order to obtain permission to come and help them. So, when I saw the dental company wishing to teach indigenous workers, and indigenous workers wishing to be trained, I invited the trainers to come to China and join our medical team.

They came multiple times and trained the local indigenous church leaders to perform dentistry at a much higher level than had been otherwise available in the region. This extra training the local church members received opened the door for their continued long-term involvement in reaching out to this unreached community. It also led to their outreach in other areas and even in establishing numerous underground house churches. It didn't seem logical to us to start a dental training program in China for local house church members. The Lord had to put that together because we otherwise would not have envisioned it. Praise God that He works in ways that we don't understand, and He still uses us to accomplish His purposes. His plans were not our plans. His plans were better (see Isaiah 55:8-9).

ACQUIRING A BUSINESS

Another example is when we started a coffee shop ministry in northwestern China. We didn't plan to start a coffee shop when we first moved to China, but it wasn't long until we began to consider it as a plan. We had learned that China was closing down many foreign NGOs because they found their work to be Christian mission-related or because they exposed or challenged aspects of the communist party that they did not wish to be made public. If our NGO were to be closed, we would no longer have a platform for a foreign visa, so we would no longer be able to work in China.

My son Andrew had studied business and has good business instincts, so he and I started to look at what business opportunities might exist for foreign workers. We did this to consider alternate routes that would support visas for foreign workers. We concluded that a coffee shop was a good opportunity because, although coffee was not a traditional Chinese drink, it was growing in popularity among the younger generation, and it was a seemingly low overhead business. It seemed that a coffee business would give opportunities for foreign workers to be welcomed in China to run the shop because of their western expertise in coffee. We studied the industry, began business plans, and actively prayed and looked at the right opportunities.

One night, Karen dreamt that she gave birth to another child (that itself would be a miracle)! But strangely, in the dream, the child was not a baby, but a toddler. And the toddler was able to walk and talk and function like a normal toddler would. Yet, it was still a baby. In the dream, we were very surprised.

Shortly after having the dream, and while not yet knowing the meaning, we were approached by a Christian man who also was a foreigner who lived in our city. We had heard about him but we had not yet met. He owned a small coffee shop and was considering selling it. It was a small shop with about six tables and 24 chairs, including one table and chairs upstairs in a small loft area that was added to the shop after it was started. We met with him to visit the shop and hear of his idea to sell it. In a matter of days, we had reached an agreement and we purchased his shop.

We interpreted Karen's dream as an encouragement of the Lord that the vision we had been pregnant with (i.e., a coffee shop in Lanzhou) was not a 'baby" but already existed and was running as a normal shop would. This gave us the encouragement to go ahead with the purchase and trust the Lord with the plan. It did not fit neatly into our overall business plan, but it was not inconsistent with it either.

We renovated the coffee shop and ran it as an adjunct to our ministry for four years. During that time, we met many wonderful Chinese friends, and many came to the Lord. The Lord used the shop to bring employment to the local Chinese and a place where the young Chinese could hear of the Lord and would be given a chance to meet Him. The loft in the upstairs of the shop sometimes served as the "upper room" as in Acts 2, where the Holy Spirit came and baptized the new Chinese believers who met Him there.

Several young Chinese believers who came to the Lord at the coffee shop later served as employees in our ministry and we remain very close to them today. Praise the Lord for how He fulfills His visions. We did hear correctly that this plan for a coffee shop was from the Lord. We were not certain exactly how it fit in with our ministry in China, but He knew. When we started moving forward with the plan by actively seeking opportunities and by listening to the Lord as He revealed a shift in the plan in the dream He gave Karen, we were able to see Him move and bring it about. We not only were able to see it bear fruit, but we were able to enjoy the fruit together. Even today we continue to keep up with our wonderful children in the Lord who came to know Him at the shop.

We have seen God do similar things as our ministry has expanded to other countries, including Russia and North Korea. His vision does not have to seem logical or consistent. He knows what He is doing and we need to trust Him.

What is your vision? What do you feel the Lord may be calling you to? Maybe you have written down your vision and feel the Lord is confirming it, but you don't know *if* and *when* you should start. Many of us have been in this same place and have asked the same questions.

You will not know the answer to all of these questions before you start. The Lord has already started leading you and is preparing the way, but He awaits you to take the next steps in front of you before you will see the next ones. Now that you have written your vision and clarified it, I would like to encourage you to let down your own nets and see what He will do. When Jesus commanded His disciples to let down their nets for a catch in Luke 5, He referred to multiple nets—plural. I believe the Lord has multiple ministries and projects for all of us! He is fully capable of multi-tasking and I think He wants to use us to our fullest capacity. His nets are endless. We need to cast them down for the catch. Your fish are waiting for you.

You might be quite surprised by the result. Doing this may begin a life-changing journey for you that will yield more fruit than you had ever envisioned before you started. You will probably experience obstacles and challenges as you move forward. Some of these may be spiritual attacks from the enemy. Some may be challenges the Lord allows so He can build your faith as you see Him work through each of them. Either way, He does have good plans and He will accomplish His purposes. This may require some unexpected changes in your vision and plan, but be flexible and allow this because He began the work and will finish it (see Philippians 1:6).

The Bible tells us that each of us have a particular role in His work. He illustrates this to us in I Corinthians 12:12-27, showing that each of us represent different parts of His body, but it is God who works all in all. And in I Corinthians 3:6-8, Paul instructs the church saying, *"I planted, Apollos watered, but God gave the increase. So then neither he who plants is anything, nor he who waters, but God who gives the increase. Now he who plants and he who waters are one, and each one will receive his own reward according to his own labor."* In God's work, each has his own part. The work that you will do for the Lord may be the result of someone else's labor and prayers, someone who has gone before you in faith. Or maybe you will be the answer to your own. Let down your nets–all of them--and let's see what He will do.

PART III

9

LIKE SERVANTS AND SPIES

> "Walk circumspectly, not as fools but as wise, redeeming the time, because the days are evil." (Ephesians 5:15-16)

> "So likewise you, when you have done all those things which you are commanded, say, 'We are unprofitable servants. We have done what was our duty to do.'" (Luke 17:10)

> "[See] that your charitable deed may be in secret; and your Father who sees in secret will Himself reward you openly." (Matthew 6:4)

IT WAS an early spring morning in Washington, D.C. I had been attending a large national pharmaceutical conference at a hotel for the past few days. This was a three-day work conference that I attended, most years, in support of my work as a pharmaceutical company lawyer, before I left this role for full-time ministry.

I faithfully attended each session and workshop to learn as much as I could. I didn't particularly enjoy the conference or find it interesting, but nonetheless, it was my job to keep abreast of the legal and regulatory developments that applied to my areas of responsibility for the company. My role was *Assistant General Counsel* and my primary job was to handle legal matters arising out of the managed care drug contracting market for the company's North American Pharmaceutical business. This meant that it was important for me to attend conferences like this one. Others from my employer-company were present at the conference, as well, which was our normal practice. This included Bob, the company vice president, who was responsible for the market-segment I served.

Bob was an interesting man. He was sharp and had good business instincts. He was also very observant. He watched people closely and was usually pretty good at understanding them and predicting their business behaviors. This is what I think made him successful in the business and why he was able to work as a senior executive of the company. He was personal, conversational, and comfortable speaking with and leading others. Although he was a bit arrogant and had a terribly foul mouth, he had good people skills, so he was able to get along with most of those he met.

I think Bob really liked me as a lawyer representing his business segment. I served him and his business purposes well by understanding the unique demands of the business and the applicable legal terrain. The pharmaceutical industry is the most regulated industry in the country, and pharmaceutical pricing is subject to many different market forces and different, and sometimes conflicting, legal and regulatory pressures. So, my expertise was valuable to him and he made sure to keep a good relationship with me, and with others in our legal department.

I got out of the taxi cab in front of the hotel early that morning. I had been staying at the conference hotel each night, and there was no reason for me to have been gone, and especially not this early in the morning. Nonetheless, I had my own agenda to fulfill, as well, which I took care of in the morning before the work day began. I had not mentioned my private agenda to anyone. It wasn't their business and I conducted it on my own time.

As I got out of the taxi in front of the hotel, Bob was also standing outside in the front of the hotel. He had gone outside after breakfast to have a quick smoke before the conference resumed for the day. He was as surprised to see me as I was to see him–because there was every reason for him to believe I was still at the hotel. There was, presumably, no other business in Washington that I needed to take care of other than his.

When I exited the taxi cab, he quickly looked over and saw that I had a stack of passports in my hand. I was holding about a dozen of them, some that were new and some that were aged and weathered. He had a perplexed look on his face as he wondered where I had been and why was I getting out of a taxi in Washington, D.C., with a stack of passports. He began to walk my way, presumably to ask what I was up to. But I could see him shirk back and instead turn to engage in conversation with another conference attendee and try to appear to ignore me as I entered the hotel and headed to my room.

Bob was convinced I was a spy. Before that day, he had told that to several of his trusted friends at the company, who also knew me and who told me what Bob had been thinking. In the past, Bob had been acquainted with others too, who may, or may not, have been government agents, so he had some basic understanding of their habits and way of life.

Bob had observed me travel for mission work, on my own time, to several former and current communist countries over the past few years—Russia, Kazakhstan, China, and North Korea. Bob was not a Christian, so he thought my Christian work was a cover for a more sinister natured work. Why would I use all of my vacation time to go to communist countries? Why would I have conducted private business in Washington so early in the morning? What was I doing with a fistful of passports?

Bob had also heard me speak in the Russian language to someone over the phone one evening when we were seated near each other during a company-sponsored business dinner. I was later told by a mutual friend that he recognized the language and that he thought I had been trained as a spy and that my work for the pharmaceutical company was a cover-identity. From that day forward, Bob was noticeably more reserved in his business interactions with me, even though I was his primary legal counsel.

I wasn't a spy. Or was I? Either way, I do love adventure, and sometimes work in the mission field is like being a spy. Not every country offers a missionary visa, and, in fact, in some countries, like China and North Korea, missionaries are not welcome. If a foreigner is to gain approval to live as a resident of the country, they must fit an approved "category" of worker, and a missionary is not one of them. That day, the passports I had in my hand belonged to my mission team. I had gone to the Chinese Embassy in Washington, D.C. that morning to get Chinese visas for our team so we could travel together.

Much of the work we do overseas has to be done in private, particularly while working in countries like China and North Korea. This does not necessarily mean that our work is illegal, but only that it must remain secretive in order to avoid suspicion that we are working in a manner that we are not otherwise approved or in a way that any given public official may not like. We have to work in our government-approved "legitimizing" field. For me, that is working as the chief representative of an NGO.

Working privately means that we have to sometimes operate openly on the matters for which we are approved to work, but more privately on those matters that are beyond the direct scope of approval. For example, if one were to hold a visa in China to run a small business, but in addition to running the business, he or she would teach a class to local Christian believers on Bible foundations, that class may be considered by some officials as *disal-*

lowed. Therefore, it would be important to operate the class independently and in private. This would also mean that you could not speak of this class, or any other side agenda, to others and you must be careful to guard the knowledge of the class by limiting involvement to only those students who fully appreciate the class. They also may hold a stake in the risk associated with a breach of the necessary confidentiality. This is not a task that you publicize to others or openly discuss as a topic of conversation about the types of work you do.

As mission workers, we have to get used to the fact that the host government is always curious about what our plans are and whether we may have a subversive agenda. We also have to get used to them covertly trying to know all that we do. This is a reasonable suspicion they have, as their role as government officials is to care for their citizens. It is reasonable for a government to seek to understand why foreigners are in their country, and it is incumbent on them to find out if foreigners are involved in secret agendas that may bring risk to the local citizenry. Sometimes, they use covert means to find out. Over the years, we have come to learn how those covert means work, and we can often see when we are being secretly followed, photographed, and videotaped by government representatives. We have become aware of other surveillance tactics.

Sometimes we see governmental-spying during our projects, such as our international medical teams. Sometimes during medical team trips, we observe that some local villagers are keen to overhear our conversations about our operations and future plans, yet they try to seem as though they are not paying attention. In one such case, one of our team members recognized an eavesdropper as an employee of the local government mayor's office. They had been sent to scout our work and to spy on us!

One time, we had been working in a Muslim village giving dental care to a very poor group of school children. We were also using this project as cover for training local Chinese house church leaders on charity work. That was the *sub-agenda* or *sub-purpose* of the team. We continued our discussions, but did so only from within parked vehicles.

At times, we have even had to close the drapes over the windows of our apartment or hotel because it is not uncommon for the government to intrude in conversations covertly by binoculars and cameras.

During one trip to the northeastern China border, I had a private evening meeting with several other ministry leaders who had traveled there to discuss a discrete project we were considering starting together. The northeastern border between China and North Korea is about a full day's journey by plane and car from our normal work territory in northwest China. The project was to begin across the border into North Korea.

Although the apartment where we met was a "safe house" and was therefore relatively secure, we were still mindful of the vulnerability of our conversations. The small town in this northeastern corner of China where we met was an area with a shared border between three countries: China, Russia, and North Korea. Because of this, it was a well-known hot-spot for tri-country espionage. Since I, as an American, was meeting in this town with leaders from South Korea and Taiwan, we were certain to be spied on. We kept the curtains closed and our voices down, and we only traveled late at night, after midnight, when no one else was likely on the road so we could be sure to monitor and know whether we were followed. Sometimes life on the field can be this way. It is a cost we need to count in deciding whether we will accept the duty and serve.

When the government sends spies to our public projects, sometimes we get an advance warning. Before one of our week-long medical team trips a few years ago, one of our local Chinese friends, who had a relative who worked for the police, gave us the heads-up that the government was going to send spies to our project because they suspected that we may be missionaries. It was very nice to get this prior warning.

We shared the warning with our team members and took extra care to assure that we did not conduct ourselves in secret, so as to raise suspicion that we are working privately with a different agenda. In fact, we were able to identify who the spies were that day, and I directly invited them to join our team and to help out in the project. They were actually delighted over this and felt more comfortable with us. I invited them to take photos and videotape our work so long as they respected patient privacy. I guess they were satisfied with what they saw and didn't feel we presented unreasonable risk because we never heard again of any fall-out from that encounter. I think they knew that we were able to identify them as government spies.

Working in the mission field can often be personally challenging. At times, it can be very lonely because, although you are surrounded by many people, you are still separated from your close friends and family. You are also separated in culture and lifestyle, which is stressful. Therefore, mission agencies like to hold meetings each year where workers from different parts of the country can come together for fellowship with each other, and they can enjoy a common bond with others who understand the similar stresses and experiences. This allows for pastoral input, mission strategy development, fellowship, and prayer.

Our organization would try to hold meetings like this each year outside the country where we worked. The reason for this was so that our meetings and conversations could remain more secure. We weren't able to hold meetings like this every year due to schedule complexities and also due to the expense for missionaries to travel outside their resident areas very often. In order to help alleviate some of the schedule complexities and travel costs, one year we decided to simply hold the meeting inside of China and try to minimize risks in other ways. It was going to be held in a small city in southern China.

I was a bit nervous about attending the meeting because we were in the process of awaiting word from the government as to whether our company's pending application for governmental re-registration had been approved. China had installed a brand-new registration scheme for NGOs like ours. It was quite unclear if many, *or even if any*, that operated like we did would be approved. So, I questioned whether it would have been wise for us to attend the meeting while awaiting word on approval since our travel to another area outside of our normal region of work would be monitored and tracked.

If, by chance, we had been monitored and tracked, we would likely later be questioned about it, and that may interfere with our registration approval and/or may bring additional undue risk to the others who also attended the meeting. This was a reasonable concern on our part because we had recently been asked by one of the Chinese government agencies we worked with about our prior travel to North Korea. So, we knew that they were spying on our travel. It was important not to raise more suspicion.

I shared my concern over this with one of my friends. He had previously served as an intelligence scout for a foreign government military agency. He confirmed my suspicion that we were being tracked and that the government likely was aware of the scheduled meeting already. He confirmed that if we had gone to the meeting, we would have been identified as having attended it. It was great to have a friend with such connections and information! Otherwise, we may have joined the meeting and experienced difficulties that could even have ended our work.

So, mission work may at times be adventuresome and it may seem like being a spy. There are times when we must be aware that we are tracked and monitored by the government and are watched by their spies. This keeps us on our toes, and we must always be aware that we are in a foreign land and our work is not appreciated by the devil. We must instead walk vigilantly in everything we do.

Ephesians 5:15-16 tells us that, as believers, we are to, *"Walk circumspectly, not as fools but as wise, redeeming the time, because the days are evil."* This applies to all believers in Jesus, not just to foreign mission workers. We are to always walk carefully knowing what the will of the Lord is. I like to think of this verse by envisioning a cat walking carefully, step by step, across the top of a concrete wall. Have you ever seen the concrete walls, especially in underdeveloped countries, that have broken glass protruding at the top? This is done, of course, to keep intruders from scaling the wall. I like to illustrate this verse by envisioning a cat carefully walking across the wall, stepping around each shard of glass, because one step could cause him to be injured or perhaps to fall off the wall completely. Every step we take, as believers, matters and we must make sure it is taken carefully.

Likewise, and importantly, every step we take in the Lord's work must be taken with the heart of a servant. Just as a spy must conduct his secret agenda in private, we must be aware that everything we do is in public, whether we like it or not. We are always being observed by others, whether that is openly or in private.

We must always have a heart to serve our Master and realize that our good deeds may at times have been in secret, too. I am referring to conducting our work to bless the Lord and to bless others in a way that does not draw attention to ourselves and what we do, but is only visible to the Lord, so He alone can get the glory. This is not always easy to do because we, naturally, like to receive credit for what we do, and sometimes it is not easy to handle when someone else seeks credit for our own work.

Jesus illustrated for us how we are to conduct our lives as His servants. In Luke 17:7-10, He explains how this plays out with us personally:

> "And which of you, having a servant plowing or tending sheep, will say to him when he has come in from the field, 'Come at once and sit down to eat'? But will he not rather say to him, 'Prepare something for my supper, and gird yourself and serve me till I have eaten and drunk, and afterward you will eat and drink'? Does he thank that servant because he did the things that were commanded him? I think not. So likewise, you, when you have done all those things which you are commanded, say, 'We are unprofitable servants. We have done what was our duty to do.'"

Whatever we do and say as a servant of the Lord is for the purpose of serving Him. It is not for the purpose of showing how good of a servant we are and how we have done great things for Him. It is important to settle this in our hearts before we ever venture out in faith and begin a new work. This is the heritage of a good servant—that our good deeds are done in secret, not public. That is what the Lord seeks from us, as He states in Matthew 6:4: *"See that your charitable deed may be in secret; and your Father who sees in secret will Himself reward you openly."*

When I was in Bible college, I was blessed to have sat under the teaching of the late Rev. Pauline Parham, who was the daughter-in-law of Dr. Charles Parham, one of the fathers of the modern Pentecostal movement. One afternoon, she gave a gripping lecture to our class on the need to walk as a servant in the ministry instead of seeking personal affirmation or recognition. At the conclusion of the lecture, she led us in a prayer to turn over to the Lord the entirety of our labor and work. Nearing the end of the prayer, she led us to pray, out loud, the following words, which continue to echo in my heart. She led us to pray that we would serve the Lord faithfully, "Even if it never becomes known, and if *someone else gets the credit."*

Do we have the heart of a servant and a spy? Do we have a

heart that works for the Master to seek the Master's favor, and His *alone*? Do we perform our works as an expression of love for our home country (heaven) and not to seek the approval or credit of its many subjects (other missionaries and friends)? Are we willing to invest all of our time, labor, money, and love in such a way that we may never be given recognition or credit by others for doing it? Are we willing to labor vigorously and consistently even if someone else who is not deserving gets the credit?

Watching someone else take credit for what we have done is easier said than done, especially when we experience it for the first time. This is something we may quickly agree to in our minds and hearts and say, "Sure, of course I would allow someone else to take credit; I am in this to please the Lord alone." But when it actually happens, I can tell you it is not easy to bear. It is especially hard when the one who is given credit for doing the work that you did not only didn't do the work, but they are happy to take the credit and act as if they had. The Lord will test us in this. He will also allow it to continue to happen so as to remind us of Who it is that we serve.

We must remember that we are "unprofitable servants" seeking to serve our Master, and not ourselves. We must remember our commitment is for His glory and not ours. If we can do this, then He knows that He can trust us with the next assignment, whatever that may bring.

I would encourage you to pray this out loud and let the Lord know, and let your own ears and heart hear:

> "Lord Jesus, I love You. I thank You that You first loved me! Thank You that You have called me to work with You and to serve Your purposes on this earth. Lord, I seek to serve You with my whole heart, holding nothing back. May I always seek Your glory and seek to bring You glory in all that I do, as an unprofitable servant who seeks the benefit of his Master alone.

> Lord, whatever You call me to, I will do. Whatever You ask me to give, I will give. Whoever You wish for me to bless, I will bless. May I always give You one-hundred percent of my labor and my love; and may I do all these for Your pleasure, even if someone else gets the credit. Amen!"

Bless you for praying this. There is nothing more satisfying in life than knowing that your service to the Lord is known by Him and appreciated by Him. It is not easy when others are credited with your work, but we remember that He is eternal. He is the one who rewards. Others may receive their reward on this earth by receiving the false approval they seek and relish. But how empty and unrewarding that must be! Yet, *you* will be rewarded in heaven–because in heaven your work is not a secret! It is known by the Lord and the "*great cloud of witnesses*" (see Hebrews 12:1) who await us when we are reunited with them in heaven forever.

10

IT DOESN'T TAKE MUCH. IT ONLY TAKES EVERYTHING.

> "Truly I say to you that this poor widow has put in more than all; for all these out of their abundance have put in offerings for God, but she out of her poverty put in all the livelihood that she had." (Luke 21:1-4)

> "And whoever does not bear his cross and come after Me cannot be My disciple.... So likewise, whoever of you does not forsake all that he has cannot be My disciple." (Luke 14:26 and 33)

THE LAND WAS IN DROUGHT. There had been no rainfall and people were suffering. Some were even dying. The lack of water affected the crops. It also affected the livestock, which didn't have the water to drink to stay healthy enough to be useful for food. This caused hardship for everyone. It impacted the farmers and it impacted the elite.

The land had gone through periods of drought before, but this time it was different. This time the drought wasn't due to the normal cycles of nature. The people could not just simply await a fresh rainfall, like they had during other periods of drought.

People were starting to sense that something else needed to change first. Rain seemed like ages away.

The land was in drought because their King had sinned. Ahab was the son of King Omri, King of Israel. Omri was an evil king and served the false gods of the region and led others to do so, as well. He reigned as King of Israel for twelve years. Ahab was his son. Therefore, Ahab was appointed to be Omri's successor. So, as Ahab grew up, he had been able to observe his father and his father's style of ruling Israel for most of his childhood and as a young adult. He probably had always lived in luxury in his father's household, and he probably thought he could do anything he wanted to do without consequence.

When Omri died, Ahab took his father's place as King, where he proceeded to commit idolatry. Ahab did not worship Jehovah. Instead, he set up altars to the false god of Baal and set up wooden images to worship him. First Kings 16:33 tells us that, *"Ahab did more to provoke the Lord God of Israel to anger than all the kings of Israel who were before him,"* —including his father King Omri. That was not a safe place to be.

The prophet Elijah knew King Ahab. He also knew Ahab's wife, Jezebel. Because of Ahab's sin against the Lord, Elijah told Ahab, *"As the Lord God of Israel lives, before whom I stand, there shall not be dew nor rain these years, except at my word"* (I Kings 17:1). Ahab probably viewed Elijah's declaration as *fighting words.* So, the Lord led Elijah away to a safe place in the wilderness and the Lord fed him there daily.

As the drought got worse and the water where Elijah had been staying dried up, the Lord told Elijah to go to Zarephath to live. The Lord told him that He had prepared a widow in Zarephath who would feed him. So Elijah traveled to Zarephath, found the widow, and asked her to provide him with some water and some bread to eat.

The widow was poor—*very* poor. The Lord had led Elijah to

the poor widow so that she could help him. But, the widow had little to offer him. In fact, the widow answered Elijah and said, *"As the Lord your God lives, I do not have bread, only a handful of flour in a bin and a little oil in a jar; and see, I am gathering a couple of sticks that I may go in and prepare it for myself and my son, that we may eat it, and die."*

Apparently, the widow of Zarephath knew she must do what the man of God asked of her. Yet, she was afraid because he seemed to ask her for all that she had. The little she did have was so scant it was not even enough to sustain her and her son.

Elijah saw her fear and answered her, *"Thus says the Lord God of Israel: the bin of flour shall not be used up, nor shall the jar of oil run dry until the day the Lord sends rain on the earth"* (I Kings 17:14). This promise from the Lord was enough for the widow. The Lord did for her exactly as He had promised. The Bible tells us that when the widow obeyed the word of the Lord, *"she and he and her household ate for many days"* (I Kings 17:15).

When the widow had first met Elijah, he challenged her faith. The Lord required something of her. The Lord required her to give *all* she had. This was very little, but nonetheless to her it was everything! All she had was enough food for *one meal* between her and her son; and God was asking her to give Him even that! This was similar to the time when Jesus recognized the poor widow who gave all she had into the offering of the temple. She gave only two "mites" which were the smallest denominated and least valuable coin in that day. Jesus recognized her sacrifice and told His disciples, *"Truly I say to you that this poor widow has put in more than all; for all these out of their abundance have put in offerings for God, but she out of her poverty put in all the livelihood that she had"* (Luke 21:1-4).

When God calls us to serve Him, He doesn't ask us for *a lot.* He only asks us for *everything.* It doesn't matter to Him if we have a little or a lot. After all, there is not much that we can have of our own that would be of much value to the Creator of all things! He simply doesn't need our stuff. But, what He does need is *our hearts.* If our hearts are attached to other things, such as our homes, cars, jobs, relationships, or any other thing that gives us comfort and a sense of stability more than Him, He will test our hearts and reveal this to us.

If we are to serve the Lord, we must be fully dependent on Him. When He tests us, sometimes He will ask us to sacrifice the very things that we feel give us the most comfort and stability. Just like He did with the widow of Zarephath when Elijah asked her to give up her very last meal with her son!

Likewise, Jesus tells us in Luke 9:23, "*If anyone desires to come after Me, let him deny himself, and take up his cross daily, and follow Me.*" This means that He wants all of us, not just part. *If* and *when* the Lord does ask us to make such sacrifices for Him and His work, He does it for our own benefit and He blesses us beyond what we would have had if we did not give what He had asked. This is exactly what took place with the widow of Zarephath, who received an endless supply of oil until the rain once again began to fall.

THE BLESSING THAT FOLLOWS SACRIFICE

I could give you numerous examples of how the Lord has asked us to make sacrifices and, when we obeyed, He blessed us beyond what we had thought. One such situation occurred early in our marriage. This experience has stood out in our hearts and has stayed with us all these years. It is a testimony He gave us so that we could remember what He can and *will* do when we obey His requests for sacrifices for Him, even when we may think that He is asking for too much.

I had just finished Bible college and I was working as an intern in the youth ministry of a local church in Texas. The church was growing quickly as many people were being saved and new members were joining every single week. For a while, it was the fastest growing church in America. Since the church was growing rapidly, the leadership began a campaign to raise funds to build a new church building that would accommodate everyone and allow room for yet more growth in the future.

We loved the church, and we wanted to help, but we did not have much to offer. I had just lost my job. I had been recovering from a bad case of hepatitis which left me unable to work for a while, Karen was pregnant with our first child, and our only car had just broken down. On top of that, rent was due soon. We were half the country away from our family. All we had in our name was about $35 cash. We were seeking the Lord and desperately asking Him for help because we needed the money to meet our bills and to eat.

That Sunday morning, I didn't expect that God would ask me to give the very little that we had. Yet, during worship I got a strong sense that the Lord was asking me to dig deep into my pocket and offer Him all we had left, to sow into His work by donating our remaining funds that very morning to the church building project. I did as I felt He had asked. I walked up to the front of the altar at the appropriate time, and I gave the Lord all that we had. It might seem that it was actually a small sacrifice since it was only $35—but to us, it was a lot. It was *everything*.

We were now left with the choice either to simply trust the Lord or to panic because we had no reserves. To be honest, it was a battle to keep positive and to trust, but it was good that we went through that and were able to see what would happen next.

We never told anyone of our financial need. We knew better. The Lord knew, and that was enough. One evening, we received a series of five visitors, one by one, each one knocking on the door of our second-floor apartment. No one knew the other was coming, and they all came at different times. None of them had talked among themselves or had heard that we had a need. In fact, I don't even think most of them knew each other. Instead, each one of our visitors had, themselves, felt that the Lord was urging them to come to our apartment and bless us. It was not coordinated by them in advance.

The first knock at our door brought us some bags of groceries. The second knock brought us a check for $200 and two boxes of food. The next knock brought us a nice lamp that they had left over from redecorating, which we actually needed for our apartment. By this time, Karen and I were looking at each other in almost disbelief and we actually began to time the intervals between these visits. The next knock brought us a frozen turkey.

The final knock on our apartment door that evening brought tears to our eyes. We had been working with the middle school-aged kids in the church youth group. We were one of two couples who had been serving as interns. Some interns worked with high school-aged kids and some with the middle schoolers. That night, two of the young middle school girls from our youth group came to see us and knocked on our door. They had been talking among themselves and felt that they wanted to bless us, so they brought us their baby-sitting money that they had been saving up. I think it was about $70.

We were shocked, and touched. The Lord had asked us to give the little we had, and we did. He blessed us in return with the resources we needed. He gave us enough money to pay rent the next week, and enough food to eat until I could return to work. Most importantly, He let us know that He had not forgotten us and that the youth we had served did not forget us either. He gave us a testimony of His faithfulness that we have been blessed to share for the rest of our lives, as I am sure the widow of Zarephath was delighted to share for the rest of her life, too!

Jesus also shows us that when He asks us to serve and when we give what little we have, He multiplies what we give and uses it for His glory and for blessing others. What we are able to give doesn't always seem like enough, but He makes it enough.

I think we all know the example in Luke 9:10-17, when Jesus was teaching the multitude, and at the end of the day, He didn't wish to send them home hungry. So, He asked His disciples to have the group sit down to feed them with the food they had to offer. They, of course, didn't have much. The Bible tells us that Jesus, *"Directed the people to sit down on the grass. Taking the five loaves and the two fish and looking up to heaven, he gave thanks and broke the loaves. Then he gave them to the disciples, and the disciples gave them to the people. They all ate and were satisfied, and the disciples picked up twelve basketfuls of broken pieces that were left over. The number of those who ate was about five thousand men, besides women and children."*

Later, after Jesus' death and resurrection, these same disciples were running the early church as recorded in the book of Acts. They had a huge responsibility. These Apostles of the Lord had all spent time very close to Jesus during His time on earth, and Jesus had poured His life into them, teaching them what they needed to know. It was their responsibility to pastor and lead the church into a new era, which they did very well.

The Lord required no less of them than He does of us. He required them to give Him *everything*, and He also required them to trust Him to multiply the little that they had.

One Sabbath, Peter and John were entering the gates of the temple. As the story goes:

> "And a man who was lame from birth was being carried to the temple gate called Beautiful, where he was put every day to beg from those entering the temple courts. When he saw Peter and John about to enter the temple, he asked them for money. Peter looked directly at him, as did John. 'Look at us!' said Peter. So, the man gave them his attention, expecting to receive something

from them. But Peter said, 'Silver or gold I do not have, but what I have I give you: In the name of Jesus Christ of Nazareth, get up and walk!'

"Taking him by the right hand, Peter helped him up, and at once the man's feet and ankles were made strong. He sprang to his feet and began to walk. Then he went with them into the temple courts, walking and leaping and praising God.

"When all the people saw him walking and praising God, they recognized him as the man who used to sit begging at the Beautiful Gate of the temple, and they were filled with wonder and amazement at what had happened to him."

The Apostles, like the common man in those days, were not people of wealth. They didn't have gold and silver that they could offer to a man who was lame. If they did, I'm guessing that they would have given him some. Yet, the Lord had them give what they did have–*which was even better!*

In China, we often pass poor and sometimes maimed beggars on the road asking help from everyone who passes by. It is nearly impossible to ignore their pitiful pleas without giving them something, even if just a little. One time, while in Beijing, I came across a man who was scarred all over his body by severe burns. Worse yet, he was missing both of his arms and both of his legs. He had been propped up against the exterior wall of a building that was next to a walkway where tourists would pass by, in hopes of donations. Unfortunately, in too many of those situations, the poor beggars are not the ones to benefit from the gifts, but those who brought them there and use them for their own gain.

But Peter and John didn't let their own personal lack stop them from offering what they actually did have–that is the power of the Holy Spirit released in faith in the name of the Lord Jesus. Although the world may not have viewed that as wealth, I am guessing that the poor man who was lame and restored to health certainly did. They only had a little to give, but it was everything.

The Lord will always stretch our faith. Sometimes He asks us to give far more than we expected that He would. Sometimes He asks us to give everything we have. He does this not to take away from us, but because it increases our capacity to receive more directly from Him. Thus, it is always for our good. Sometimes we have to empty our hearts of *things* (things of comfort and security) so that He can refill our hearts with that which is eternal (His love, peace, and joy).

The Lord always expects us to share what we have. First John teaches, "*If anyone has material possessions and sees a brother or sister in need but has no pity on them, how can the love of God be in that person?" (I John 3:17).* Sometimes, others need to see the act of love on our part to know that He loves them. He doesn't require us to hand over much, but only everything. Are you ready to do so? I'm not asking you to. But perhaps *He* is asking you. He will ask you not only to agree, but He'll ask you to express your willingness of heart by making a sacrifice. He will test that, and it may come in ways you didn't expect.

11

HE USES EVERYTHING, BECAUSE "IT IS FINISHED"

> "And we know that all things work together for good to those who love God, to those who are called according to His purpose." (Romans 8:28)

> "Come and see the works of God, who is awesome in His deeds toward the sons of men." (Psalm 66:5)

IT IS AMAZING how God tailors the details of our lives and uses everything in our lives, past and present. Usually He does this without our knowing or expecting it. He uses experiences that we never thought were relevant or applicable to establish our destiny and fulfill it. We can only look back in amazement to see what He has done.

I mentioned before how it came about that Dr. Art joined our medical team. He had been working out at the hospital fitness center while meditating on Romans 8:28, when Karen's nurse-friend asked him if he wished to join. When I reflect back on how the Lord put all of this ministry together, the experience of how He invited Dr. Art to join us was a major catalyst.

Romans 8:28 is a commonly learned and quoted scripture, *"And we know that all things work together for good to those who love God, to those who are called according to His purpose."* We often fall back to this verse, rightly I might add, when we experience loss or disappointment, or face situations we didn't wish for or cannot explain. We also rely on this truth when we experience our own failures and hope that God will perhaps re-engineer facts to make them, or make us, whole.

What was the Lord communicating to Dr. Art when he was meditating on Romans 8:28? To Dr. Art, the message from the Lord through this verse was clear. When the nurse asked him if he wished to come, his heart was prepared and he instantly said, "Yes."

But what did this verse mean for our ministry that he joined? Or perhaps yours? What does it mean for the circumstances of your life that, for now, may seem to be inconsistent with your vision or perhaps may have hindered or delayed it? How may this verse apply to situations that have caused you setback and may have left you with a feeling that you have been deprived of your rightful destiny in the Lord? Maybe these situations have left you with questions of whether you may never experience or achieve what you, and He, wished that you would. Perhaps these situations may have been your, or someone else's, fault?

These are all good, viable questions. The answers to all these questions will be personal ones between you and the Lord. I have learned that Romans 8:28 is a great statement of God's covenant with His people. It is a promise that when we have a relationship with Him, He loves us, He is committed to us, and He is ever at work in and through us. It is a declaration that He did not create us to be a disconnected experiment or a fleeting hope. He is always with us. He knew what He was doing, He deliberately made plans for our lives individually, and He is ever-determined to fulfill His plans.

Romans 8:28 tells us that no matter what we experience in life, and perhaps no matter what problems we may have caused ourselves and/or others—our God is a God of redemption. That is His nature. Although He does not wish such negative and hurtful things, or things that seemingly may thwart His plan for our lives, Romans 8:28 tells us that these things are not the final picture. It demonstrates to us that the hope we have is not fleeting, but is *real*. It tells us what we cannot do ourselves, God can do Himself. Praise the Lord for this!

When Jesus was being crucified, God was fulfilling His Word and establishing His covenant of salvation for us eternally. After the agony that Jesus suffered on the cross, and immediately before He died, He declared, out loud, the words, *"It is finished!"* (see John 19:30). Jesus' declaration, "It is finished," originates from the Hebrew word *tetelestai*. This word carries the meaning of finality and completion, such as the final payment and release of a debt. Importantly, *tetelestai* appears in the *perfect tense* meaning that it applies in the past, present, and future, all together. When Jesus died, the payment for our sin was finished. Our debt was paid in full—past, present, and future.

Jesus' act of *tetelestai* released His covenant throughout eternity beyond the stretches of time. It released Romans 8:28 to us as a testimony that He can and does stretch across time to engineer past, present, and future, for His glory and for the good of those who love Him and are called by Him. This means that no matter the circumstances we wrestle with and no matter what we may have done or failed in doing, He is still at work and will use these things for our good. He knew our weaknesses, circumstances, and failures before we even did.

So, because of His *tetelestai*–His payment of our sin and establishing a covenant with us—He has been at work engineering our lives in the past, present, and future for His purposes. It is never too late for anything because His covenant has been established forever! With that in mind, I encourage you to read the passage again: "*All things [now] work together for good to those who love God, to those who are called according to His purpose" (Romans 8:28).*

I had felt early in my life that God had a special plan for my life. I was right. He did, and He has a special plan for yours, too. Yet, it seemed that my life took a different turn. The demands of career, family, and others' expectations, and perhaps my own decisions, seemed to send me in a different direction than what I perceived God had destined. Although this seemed true, God still used all of these to actually fulfill His destiny in my life instead of derailing it.

The Lord demonstrated Romans 8:28 to me when I only had a vision and hope that He would use me and begin a new ministry to be a *pathway to hearts.* I had a hope of His destiny, but I had no resources or experiences to draw from. Dr. Art's phone call was the catalyst of it all. It was his phone call that gave me the evidence the Lord was in the plan, that He was at work, and that what I could not do, He could. I didn't know any doctors, but now a doctor was reaching out to me. *And he was reaching out to me with the very verse—Romans 8:28!*

What will be your Romans 8:28 moment? I cannot tell you when it will come, but I can tell you that when you move forward in the Lord, leaving your failures, hurtful experiences, or unexpected and undeserved delays in the past, your Romans 8:28 moment will come because He is indeed at work in engineering these experiences to work your good.

The Lord will begin to show you that His hand was at work the whole time. It began before you knew it. He will show you that the experiences you have had and situations you have endured (or perhaps caused) are useful for the very destiny that seems lately to have become an image in the rearview mirror moving farther and farther away. He will show you how the little things throughout your life made you uniquely qualified for the work He called you to do—and that only He can do that.

How could this be, if the little things that He will use are things that He didn't will to happen? If these little things moved me *away* from the destiny of His call, then how are these things going to help me to fulfill it as though they were part of the plan?

The answer is Romans 8:28. God is faithful to use these things in a way that only He can. We learn that these things didn't stop His work. What can stop God from achieving His purposes? Nothing can. Not even time. We can make poor decisions and delay or impede His will in our lives, but if we let Him, He will use everything and His purposes will be established. Take His promise for this.

THE FATHER'S HEART

As I shared earlier, when I was younger, I had sensed that the Lord or His angel had been watching me and had a plan for my life. I had hopes and dreams to be a doctor or scientist. I think the Lord was at work preparing me for a medical mission ministry, even though the route I would later take toward that vision was not a direct one.

Life then came. Bills needed to be paid. Babies were on the way and expectations were high. Did I abort His plans when I left the part-time youth ministry to return to college, law school, and a secular career? I'm not completely sure. But I am sure that I didn't think I'd walk in His destiny after that. I thought it was over. I didn't know that God was already tailoring the things in my career and parenthood (the things that I allowed to take me away from ministry) to actually bring me into a place of ministry, and in a greater portion that I could have had if I had progressed along the pathway I was on to begin with.

Had I continued studying ministry and following a career path of ministry, I may not have been able to live, or perhaps even travel to countries tightly closed to the Gospel, as I do now. Nor would I have been able to enter into the medical mission ministry from a position of strength like I could do now.

Since I instead traveled the long career route of a healthcare lawyer, I gained a wealth of experience in the administration of health services. I had represented the whole scope of healthcare providers from multi-institutional healthcare providers to individual practitioners. I represented a major pharmaceutical company and thus understood medicine in a very deep way. I had previously served as an emergency medical technician and a hospital emergency room technician. I had personally suffered some fairly major medical setbacks and chronic conditions that, all in their own right, could have disqualified me from serving in ministry overseas.

All of these things which I thought *took me away* from the ministry actually became not only valuable for the medical mission work in the unreached lands, but they were what *actually* made it possible. Without these, I could not have done this and this ministry would not have arisen. God used the alternative path that I thought moved me away from the ministry He called me to, to instead make the ministry possible and activate my destiny instead of extinguishing it.

He also used my career to open doors or relationships that even enhanced the ministry, such as gaining relationships with other healthcare organizations to obtain donations of vaccines, medicines, and medical supplies for large-scale outreach. He used my experiences as a lawyer in serving clients where I learned to help make their way successful only to see them take the credit for it. He used this to prepare me and my own heart to be equipped for a ministry that works in the shadows where no one can see or give us credit. I had to learn to be pleased with others receiving approval and taking credit for successes even when they were really my own.

I became a father at a relatively young age. Karen and I married when I was twenty-one years old and she was eighteen, and we had our first baby when I was twenty-three. Three more children came shortly thereafter. I had a lot to learn about fatherhood. I wanted to be a good dad, but at twenty-three I was not sure how to manage what I had envisioned my role should have been. Learning to be a dad was not an easy task for me. Today, each of my four children love the Lord and serve Him actively. The Lord is gracious!

As I learned to be a dad while raising my own family, He used this experience to help me understand what His orphans lack. I was able to recognized God more deeply for the wonderful father that He is to me. Not just to others, but even to me! I learned that, what I lacked in my understanding of God as a father to me, was lacking in yet a more significant way in those who never had a dad, or mom, to model after, to receive love from, and to know the unconditional father's love. This transformation in our own hearts must take place for us to walk in a ministry to bring love and blessing to orphans. We must first understand what they needed the most, and know how to help meet that need. If we don't know God's heart as our father, how can we help others to?

God will use everything. He will use your heartaches, your failures, your successes, and your pain. He will use what you thought was insignificant and what perhaps you thought was lost forever. He will amaze you with how He will bring those things not only to develop you along the pathway of His destiny for your life, but He will bring you to the place where you can look back and see how those things surprisingly were necessary to bring you to the place of destiny instead of moving you away from it forever. Only He can do this. Romans 8:28 is a great truth of the covenant of our God that He will use "all things," not just "some things," for good, for those who love Him and are called according to His purpose.

12

FINAL WORDS OF WISDOM

"For wisdom is better than rubies, and all the things one may desire cannot be compared with her." (Proverbs 8:11)

"The silver-haired head is a crown of glory, If it is found in the way of righteousness.... Wisdom is with aged men, And with length of days, understanding." (Proverbs 16:21 and Job 12:12)

TODAY, our ministry continues in several countries. Our international base is in the United States and our primary projects are in the rural, unreached communities in northwest China. We have a staff of seven full-time and part-time workers, and we host hundreds of volunteers each year. Each time, we have felt our ministry may become limited due to external pressures (such as governmental changes, etc.); somehow, miraculously, He expands our work and influence.

The Lord is kind and He is always teaching us new things. This is His nature as a teacher (see John 13:13). In ministry, I am always learning new things, and as circumstances in my life arise, my normal thought processes and preconceived ideas are challenged.

It is always good to pause and to reflect on what we have learned and how we may share what we have learned with others. If wisdom is valuable, which it is according to Proverbs 3:14-24, then why would we want it to go to waste and not share it with others—and especially with our children? I would like to share with you some specific, unique things that the Lord has taught me. These have been personal to me, but perhaps He may speak to you about these areas, as well.

FINISH WHAT YOU START: A LESSON ON FAITHFULNESS

"Let your 'Yes' be 'Yes.'" (Matthew 5:37)

When my family and I began to build our house together, there were more tasks, nuances, and details than I could have ever imagined. I did not realize how complicated even the smallest details could be. Each task always seemed to lead to another task that we had not expected, and almost every one of them took more time and sometimes caused more delays and additional purchases than we had planned or budgeted for. Even the simple task of cutting around the corners of each piece of wall trim and door trim required additional tools. It sometimes took numerous attempts before I got it right.

After we moved into the home, there was still a lot of work we needed to do to complete it. We continued to work on these things after we re-started our normal daily life. However, after a while, we left certain tasks on hold to complete later. For example, we had a palladium window at the top of our foyer which would have required us to rent scaffolding so we could climb up and finish the trim. So, it stayed unfinished. Since no one would likely notice the incomplete trim, we just decided not to do it. This was true of several tasks in the overall house. Although we were living in the house as normal life allowed, the job was still unfinished. When we sold the house and prepared to move out, all of these tasks finally had to be done in order to satisfy the buyers. I asked myself, "Why didn't we finish them to begin with and enjoy the finished project while we still lived there?"

Ministry projects are the same. They usually lead to more commitment and involvement than we had anticipated or envisioned before we started. Some of those details require more funds, more time, and more delay than we otherwise think are necessary or reasonable. Some tasks may require us to re-order our priorities in order to complete, or not complete them. It is easy to get discouraged and to leave certain things undone or to even put the entire ministry or project on hold until it is a more convenient time in our lives to engage with it.

I have observed some ministries and ministry projects where the servant of the Lord receives His call and eagerly begins to walk in what he or she believes God has spoken to them. When hardships and challenges arise and persist, or perhaps simply the pressures of daily life, the ministry and projects go on hold and are sometimes never completed. This, I think, is often a bad testimony. I am guilty of this, too. I have learned the need to persist with a thing to its conclusion, or until the time that the Lord may release me to stop.

The Lord usually does not call us to begin His work and then leave it up in the air. Consider the story of when Jesus was teaching His disciples and He asked them to travel by boat across the Sea of Galilee to the other side (Matthew 28:23-27). The storm arose and they were afraid. When they frantically woke the Lord up from a nap in the boat to help them, He rebuked the storm and they then came to the other side as originally planned. The Lord did not call them to stay drifting in water or to turn back and return to where they began. Instead, they completed the journey to the planned destination.

When you begin a work for the Lord, it is incumbent on you to complete it, unless you are relieved of the responsibility by Him. It is sometimes better not to begin a project than to begin it and leave it unfinished. It is important that you obey His voice and begin His work and let your "yes" be "yes" when you answer the Lord's call. You also must not enter a place of indecisiveness or double-mindedness. This not only leaves God's call undone, causing the results to stall or stop, but leaves a bad impression on those who may observe and follow.

Jesus taught that it is better to carefully plan and evaluate what is needed to finish a project before you commit to begin it. In Luke 14:28-33, Jesus said, "*For which of you, intending to build a tower, does not sit down first and count the cost, whether he has enough to finish it — lest, after he has laid the foundation, and is not able to finish, all who see it begin to mock him, saying, 'This man began to build and was not able to finish'? Or what king, going to make war against another king, does not sit down first and consider whether he is able with ten thousand to meet him who comes against him with twenty thousand? Or else, while the other is still a great way off, he sends a delegation and asks conditions of peace. So likewise, whoever of you does not forsake all that he has cannot be My disciple.*"

The Lord tells us that once we have started to obey Him we should not look back. In Luke 17:31-34, when He was speaking of the coming of the day of the Lord, Jesus said, "*In that day, he who is on the housetop, and his goods are in the house, let him not come down to take them away. And likewise the one who is in the field, let him not turn back.*" He then reminded His disciples about Lot's wife (verse 32), who at the time of God's judgment of Sodom and Gomorrah turned to look back and was turned into a pillar of salt. Furthermore, in Luke 9:62, Jesus said, "*No one, having put his hand to the plow, and looking back, is fit for the kingdom of God.*" This is a reference to a person's decision to follow Christ and then turn back to his or her old life. It shows the Lord's desire that when we say "yes" to Him, we should not look back and change our mind.

It is important that when we begin a task, we don't look back and wonder if maybe we would prefer not to have started it. We need to set our hearts to complete it. Undertaking a ministry task, no matter how small or how large, is not a light thing. It is an eternal work with eternal consequences. It must be considered, started, and executed with a heart of faithfulness to Him and the duty He has laid on our hearts to perform. The Lord calls us to be faithful in what He has asked us to do (Luke 16:12-14). There are times that the Lord may relieve us of a task, but that should not be considered lightly. This should be considered in prayer and good counsel of other leaders in the body of Christ.

Personally, if I had properly evaluated how much time, resources, commitment, and frustration building my own home would have required, I would have hired the project out to a builder and would not have tried to do it myself. But, I learned. In the end, we had a nice home to live in. I am not suggesting that you decline the invitation of the Lord to agree with Him and begin His work. I am only counseling you to count the cost of your obedience to begin it, so that you will have the commitment to complete the work you have begun. Once you have begun the work, have the same mind as the Lord, namely, *"He who has begun a good work in you will complete it"* (Philippians 1:6).

A "BALANCED" LIFE CAN BECOME A LIFE WITHOUT PASSION

We have all learned in school that it is important to eat a balanced diet in order to stay healthy. If we only eat those things that we wish to eat, when we wish to eat them, we might be okay for a while, but we would soon lose strength and eventually suffer greater health consequences. Instead, from time to time, we can enjoy sweets and other things that may not be as healthy as other foods, but this must be in moderation and not the totality of our diet.

So, too, is our spiritual life. We must maintain a balanced spiritual diet. We cannot thrive spiritually by only taking in limited doses of Scripture on select topics we prefer or to limit our prayers to personal needs and things we want God to do for us. Those are all good things—but, they are not, and should not be considered the totality of our spiritual diet. We need to pursue the Lord and learn His Scriptures, even the ones we may think are boring or inapplicable, because they, too, are treasures.

I'd like to share insights I've learned about living an overall balanced life from day-to-day, as Christians. Specifically, I am talking about the tasks of service, leadership, and ministries that we should all take part in to serve the Kingdom.

I have learned that, personally, I just can't do it all. I simply *can't*... and I have tried. There are many false responsibilities that we, as followers of Jesus, are led to believe are necessary in order for us to be good examples as His children and lead a "balanced" Christian life. I would like to ask you to consider something that I have shared with many others: *a balanced life can become a life without passion.*

What!? Did I really say that? Yep, I did. Here is what I mean. All of us have only a finite amount of time and energy in any given day, week, month, year, and lifetime. What are we going to do with our time? What are we going to do with our energy? What we do with our time and energy is our own decision and we are solely accountable to the Lord for those decisions.

I believe that the Lord has special plans and callings for each of us. Some of these may seem large, and some may seem small. In the Lord's eyes, these are never small, and His rewards to us for obeying and completing His requests are based solely on whether we have been faithful (Matthew 25:21).

All of us probably have heard, "God has a wonderful plan for your life" —and He does. *But*, sadly, so does everyone else! It seems everyone else has a plan for my life, too.

Throughout life, many others, usually innocently, have preconceived ideas of what we, personally, must do to be faithful to the Lord. Even though they are not the ones who are accountable for our decisions and our faithfulness.

We see this play out by the long list of duties and acts of service that we are so often asked or expected to perform, in order to have a "balanced" Christian life. In frustration, I once sat down and made a list of all these things I felt others think I am responsible to do in order to have a "balanced" Christian life and to be a faithful servant of the Lord. The list, in part, included:

Attend church	Join a Men's group
Attend Sunday School	Join a Bible study
Teach Sunday School	Become a mentor
Join a small group	Tithe
Attend Sunday night or midweek church meeting	Donate
Join the church picnic	Sponsor a missionary
Join the church prayer group or prayer meetings	Sponsor an orphan child
Always have morning devotions	Pay for someone's mission trip
Pray for the missionaries	Fundraise
Go on a mission trip	Read at least one book every month
Lead a mission trip	Read through the Bible in one year
Local outreach to the poor	Keep a journal of everything that happens
Attend a marriage seminar	Listen to Christian radio when you drive
Go to marriage counseling	Pray when you drive
Go on the church retreat	Listen to Christian teaching tapes when you drive
Take the kids to youth group	Make sure you take care of your "temple": eat right and exercise
Chaperone a youth group trip	Get plenty of sleep
Attend Christian concerts	Spend lots of time with your spouse
Be involved in a ministry or committee	Go away for the weekend with your spouse
Bring friends to crusades and revivals	Go to the Christmas and Easter programs
Organize prayer meetings at work	Write encouraging notes to others

This list of "expectations" includes wonderful things. In fact, they are all good. Many times, the Lord does call us to some or maybe even all of these things. Of course, others may often be quick to point out when we fail to do some or all of these, too. Sometimes we may hold ourselves accountable for performing these. Perhaps you can relate to this?

The fact is, we probably do not have time for all of these things if we are going to be faithful to the Lord and complete what He actually has asked us to do *individually*. If we try to do it all, I submit to you, we may be undertaking *false responsibilities* that we have not received from the Lord. Because of this, it is important that we prayerfully consider each and every offer of service before we accept it. Otherwise, your expense of energy toward these *good* tasks will zap your emotional energy and passion from those things God has especially engaged in your heart.

One exception to this that I have learned is that, regardless of what we may think is otherwise important, the Lord has created us in such a way that necessitates that we observe His Sabbath. There is a reason God created the world in six days and He rested on the seventh. He expects us to rest also. As Derek Prince used to say, "If we don't take the Sabbath, the Sabbath will take us." We could try for a while to work without His Sabbath rest, and of course there are situations that arise that we must respond to, but if we make it a habit of neglecting to observe the Sabbath, there will be a heavy price to pay.

I learned this the hard way. As a lawyer, I learned that working on weekends was necessary, and I continued that pattern when I left my employment for ministry. In fact, there was rarely a single day in the week that I did not devote some, or sometimes *all,* of the day to work, instead of to rest and family. I burned out physically and emotionally. I lost a considerable and unhealthy amount of weight without a medical explanation, and my daily investment of time to His work began to have decreasing, marginal returns. Only after I committed to observe His Sabbath was I able to regain momentum. I learned that when we observe the Sabbath, we can accomplish seven days' worth of work in six days, but we cannot accomplish it in seven.

Passion is good. God wants us to be passionate about Him and passionate for His work. But if we try to do everything that seems *spiritual* and *good,* we cannot maintain our passion for what He has called us to. As a result, we may even lose our passion for Him—which is tragic! Instead, we will be reduced to having a performance mentality of achieving important ministry tasks simply because we are "supposed" to do them, and not because He has prepared us and empowered us by our unique design and abilities. In this, our excitement of walking by faith to see Him act on our behalf will suffer (see II Chronicles 16:9). A quest to live a so-called "balanced life" could lead us to live a life without passion for the true aspects of His work that He has called us to be faithful to perform.

Sometimes the work of ministry is hard enough, and to lose our passion for it would make it yet harder. Stay focused on what He has called you to do, and don't let the enemy steal your passion by making you feel obligated to also focus on other things that are seemingly good, especially to others. Many times, those things will only serve to distract you and steal your emotional energy. Let Him ignite your heart with passion for Him and for His work, and let Him empower you to finish His work.

SPIRITUAL WARFARE IS WARFARE!

I had been invited to enter the room. I knew the room was significant, but I didn't know why. I felt I didn't have a choice, but that didn't seem to matter at all. I had such an impending sense of the importance of the moment—a sense of reverence, holy fear, and excitement, all wrapped up together. So, I entered.

I was dreaming. Really, I was. I had this dream the first night I ever spent in China. I did not yet have a clear direction or assignment from the Lord and I did not yet know that He was about to birth a ministry with such purpose that the next twenty years of our lives would be spent "holding on for dear life" as He led us and unfolded our destiny. I only knew that I had been invited to bring a team to China and that I was going ahead to China in advance so that I could understand the mission and prepare the way.

In the dream, the angel of the Lord had appeared. He was

strong and majestic. I felt that whatever it was that the Lord had called me to do was something this angel could certainly do himself with both hands tied behind his back, but that wasn't important or relevant. There was some business to take care of and the Lord had sent His angel to perform it, and now was the time.

The angel led me into the room. All four walls of the room were filled with racks that contained swords. Each sword was hanging on the racks vertically. They were not organized by size or shape. Instead they were organized by a certain purpose and design that I find hard to put into words. It was as though each sword had a unique use and purpose, and that purpose was somehow apparent to me in the dream through an indescribable nature or essence that the swords each inherently held.

I examined the swords, but I knew I had to choose one. I knew that the one I would choose is the one that I would have to learn to use. I walked mid-way down the first rack on the left wall. I picked up a few of them to examine them, but very shortly after I chose one in particular. It was smaller than most, but it had an essence about it that would make it unique to me. I knew I could use it in warfare, for the purpose it was designed.

I have thought about this dream so many times throughout the years as this ministry has unfolded. I believe that the Lord had prepared me for the ministry He was birthing and for work ahead. But this last task was to equip me to handle the battles that were ahead, so that I could win them! He gave me His sword.

We have experienced many spiritual battles in the ministry. That happens as a regular course as we move forward with God's assignments. Usually, spiritual battles don't announce themselves. They often come when we least expect them and in ways we did not expect, and they sometimes take us off balance. The Word of God tells us, *"We do not wrestle against flesh and blood, but against principalities, against powers, against the rulers of the darkness of this age, against spiritual hosts of wickedness in the heavenly places*" (Ephesians 6:12).

To win these battles, we need to be equipped with His spiritual armor and His spiritual weapons. We must know the Word of God and we must learn how to use it in spiritual battle. Our battles are unseen, but the Lord has equipped us with His sword for battles. Second Corinthians 10:4-6 tells us that tells us, "*The weapons of our warfare are not carnal but mighty in God for pulling down strongholds, casting down arguments and every high thing that exalts itself against the knowledge of God, bringing every thought into captivity to the obedience of Christ, and being ready to punish all disobedience when your obedience is fulfilled.*" And the Lord tells us that we overcome the devil, "*By the blood of the Lamb and by the word of [our] testimony*" (Revelation 12:11). The Lord has equipped each believer with these weapons and they are necessary for us to engage in *and win* the fight.

One afternoon, we were mid-way through one of our week-long medical teams in a very unreached Muslim village in north-western China. Our team was busy caring for the poor, but as the leader of the team, I had some flexibility in my time to observe and pray. I decided I would walk to an adjacent hill where I could overlook the whole medical team at work so that I could pray for them. So, I left the site to climb the hill.

I prayed for the team and asked God to bless each one and to make His name known. I didn't stop there. I then started taking authority over the enemy and commanding the devil to give back all the territory we stood on and for him to flee that place. I felt like Joshua when, after Moses' death, the Lord told him, "*Every place that the sole of your foot will tread upon I have given you*" (Joshua 1:3). So, I declared that God had given this land to us, and I told the enemy, the devil, to disembark and flee.

I felt good about my spiritual warring, but I was not prepared for what happened next. As I was standing there, I felt a hard *punch* into my stomach as if a person had been standing in front of me and coldly sucker-punched me in the gut. I doubled over forward. When I did, I felt another punch from behind. It was as if someone standing behind me punched me in the kidney. *What is happening?* I was getting hit and punched and no one was even around me!

I had engaged the enemy and picked a fight with him. But, I wasn't ready for him to react and retaliate. Certainly not like this. I retreated to the team and joined together in prayer with some of our other team members until we sensed the Lord's victory. I learned that it wasn't helpful to just choose the battles I wanted to fight on a whim and expect a quick victory. I learned that all of our projects for the Lord must be individually bathed in prayer and fasting, and we must be ready, prayerfully, to use His spiritual weapons to win the battles once they have begun.

We need to learn to declare the Word of God in active battle against the devil. In Luke 10:19, Jesus tells us, *"Behold, I give you the authority to trample on serpents and scorpions, and over all the power of the enemy, and nothing shall by any means hurt you."* This authority is our heritage! In Hebrews 2:14, He tells us that, *"Through death He [destroyed] him who had the power of death, that is, the devil."* When we declare His Word verbally, we are releasing our faith and using the Word as an offensive weapon against the devil, who is already defeated.

To win spiritual battles, we must learn to put on the whole armor of God, as Paul instructed us in Ephesians 6:11 and 14-17: *"Put on the whole armor of God that you may be able to stand against the wiles of the devil... Stand therefore, having girded your waist with truth, having put on the breastplate of righteousness, and having shod your feet with the preparation of the gospel of peace; above all, taking the shield of faith with which you will be able to quench all the fiery darts of the wicked one. And take the helmet of salvation, and the sword of the Spirit, which is the word of God."*

Personally, when I enter into a place of spiritually battling with the enemy, I will put on the armor of God by verbally declaring each of these pieces of armor and the nature of the Lord that each reflects. I will say:

> "Lord, I gird my loins with truth because You are the Truth (John 14:6). I put on the breastplate of righteousness because Jesus has been made unto me righteousness (I Corinthians 1:30). I shod my feet with the preparation of the Gospel of peace because You have called me to readiness and You are my peace (Ephesians 2:14). Above all, I take up the shield of faith with which I shall quench all the fiery darts of the enemy (Psalm 3:3). I take up the sword of the Spirit, which is the Word of God (Revelation 19:15)."

I then claim the blood of the Lord Jesus as a spiritual weapon. The Lord tells us in Revelation that we overcame the devil, "*By the blood of the lamb and by the word of [our] testimony,*" so we can claim His blood as an offensive weapon in faith.

By verbally declaring His Word, we are verbally agreeing with the Word of God and we are releasing our faith. Our ears and our hearts hear His Word and it builds our faith further to actively protect us in the battles and to beat the devil.

The battle is the Lord's, but it is a battle. The war is won, but it still must be fought before we can experience the victory that He has already won. The war is spiritual, but we have spiritual weapons. We must learn to use them and we must always keep in mind that the enemy does attack, so when he does attack, we are not surprised and taken off guard, but instead are in a position to use the weapons, the swords, He has equipped us with and trained us to use.

REMEMBER THE ORPHANS, WIDOWS, AND STRANGERS

The heart of the Lord is for the weak. Perhaps this is best displayed by the very act of the Lord coming from His place of majesty in heaven, to the earth, to Himself take our place and bear the punishment we deserved. Romans 5:6 tells us, *"For when we were still without strength, in due time Christ died for the ungodly."*

The Lord encourages us to be like Him to reach out to and help those who are otherwise unable to care for themselves. James 2:14-17 says, *"What does it profit, my brethren, if someone says he has faith but does not have works? Can faith save him? If a brother or sister is naked and destitute of daily food, and one of you says to them, 'Depart in peace, be warmed and filled,' but you do not give them the things which are needed for the body, what does it profit? Thus, also faith by itself, if it does not have works, is dead."*

Throughout the Word of God, we see God's heart for certain people who by their severe situations are vulnerable and especially in need of help. As we discussed, the Lord gives special status to orphans, widows, and strangers (see Deuteronomy 10:18-19; Psalm 68:5). This is because they are in compromised positions in life and need the help of others to make it. Job 29:12 tells us that the Lord, *"Delivered the poor who cried out, the fatherless and the one who had no helper."* Psalm 68:5 says God Himself is, *"A father of the fatherless, a defender of widows."* James 1:27 adds, *"Pure and undefiled religion before God and the Father is this: to visit orphans and widows in their trouble, and to keep ones-self unspotted from the world."*

Each of us will have different ministries with varying focuses. This is all good because the body of Christ is diverse and all of our gifts are necessary (I Corinthians 12:12-21). Some of these ministries are called to have a direct impact on orphans, widows, and strangers, and some are not.

I have observed and learned that, regardless of the focus of our respective ministries, the Lord has emphasized that His heart closely regards those who are in these special status positions. If we take heed and care to help them, we are blessing those who are very close to His own heart. He not only regards this highly but He blesses us for it (see Deuteronomy 14:29; Jeremiah 7:6-7).

I am not suggesting that we independently change the focus of what God has called us to do, to instead focus on orphans and widows. However, I am encouraging the reality that each of us has a responsibility to the Lord to care for the things He cares about, and orphans and widows are ones close to His heart. Therefore, it would serve us well to serve them well. He loves them! So we should love them, too. I would encourage you to look for opportunities in your life to serve orphans and widows, and those who do not have the strength or position to care for themselves. Your Father in heaven will be honored if you do.

I sincerely hope that these stories and exhortations can help you in your journey of understanding your call from the Lord and your responsibility of walking in it. The work of the Lord is a serious work and it is a joy to be partakers with the Lord as laborers in His harvest. And I, personally, am especially joyful for the opportunities that arise when I can share with others the unique things I have learned. I encourage you to do the same.

PRAYER OF SALVATION

Dear Jesus,

I come before You now because I need You and I desire to have a personal relationship with You. I know that I am a sinner and that I cannot save myself. I am ready for You to be my Savior and my Lord.

I thank You that You are God's Son. I thank You that You came into the world and led a sinless life. You bore my sins in Your body, You died on the cross, and God raised You up from the dead. I thank You that this was Your divine plan from the beginning.

I come to You now and ask You to please forgive me for all of my sins. Forgive me for living my own life my own way. I ask You now to be the Lord of my life, completely. I ask You to please come into my heart and make me Your child, so that I can live with You forever. I receive You now as my Savior and as the Lord of my life.

Thank You, Jesus, for being my Lord. Please teach me about You, teach me Your ways, and help me to live my life for You.

Amen.

ABOUT THE AUTHOR

MIKE KASTLE is a servant of the Lord called to minister to unreached people in closed countries. He currently resides both in the United States and in China. The nature of his work requires privacy for reasons of security, so the name Mike Kastle is a pseudonym so as to maintain anonymity. Mike's true identity is kept private for the time being.

Made in the USA
Middletown, DE
27 August 2020

17187382R00104